Rugged Discipleship

Show Me Your Friends, I Will Show You Your Future

By
Steve Connor

Overwhelming Victory Press
Canton, Ohio
Copyright © 2020, Steve Connor
ISBN: 978-1-7345001-0-3

General Editor Dr. Greg Linville, CSRM International
P. O. Box 9110 Canton, OH 44711

Email: sportsminresources@gmail.com
Scripture quotations are from the
English Standard Version of the Bible.

Other Books by the Author

- *Sports Plus: Handbook on Sports Youth Ministry* (Wesley Owens Publications, 1998)
- *Sports Outreach Topical Bible* (W. G. Thiessen, Cross Training Publications, 1999)
- *A Sporting Guide to Eternity* (Christian Focus Publications, 2002)
- *Sports Outreach: Principles and Practices of Successful Sports Ministry* (Christian Focus Publications, 2003)
- *Discovery Teams* (Christian Focus Publications, 2004)
- *Impact Teams* (Christian Focus Publications, 2004)
- *Leadership Teams* (Christian Focus Publications, 2004)
- *NT: Sport—Europe, The Word of God for the World of Sport* (Scottish Bible Society, 2004)
- *NT: Sport—USA, The Word of God for the World of Sport* (Tyndale Publishing, 2004)
- *Power: NT, South Pacific Sports New Testament* (Australian Bible Society, 2005)
- *Coaching Character* (Open Source, 2008)

Dedication

To Hayleigh:
wife, mother, missionary.

Proverbs 13:20
"Whoever walks with the wise becomes wise..."

Table of Contents

Praise for Rugged Discipleship

Knowing Steve for nearly 30 years, I have personally seen him live out this concept—Rugged Discipleship. His middle name is discipleship! I traveled with him around the world, and witnessed his investment in leaders to become discipleship-makers. This book is a readymade guide for anyone who wants to understand the Biblical view of discipleship. My favorite one word for this book is MUST! You MUST read it today, and discover how to be a rugged follower of Jesus Christ who can have Kingdom impact!

Dan Britton, Chief Field Office for Fellowship of Christian Athletes, and Author of six books, including *One Word*

Love this book! As a young athlete in a completely new world, I made the transition from Texas to Indiana. Being lost on campus and on the football field, a place at Mama C's dinner table, enjoying amazing meals, was when I often felt at home. After my belly was full, I was able to gain a spiritual fill by conversing with Mr. Steve. As my spiritual coach in college, and now an influence on my life, I know one thing. Mr. Steve radiates love: love for God, and love for seeing God shine through men.

Dimitric Camiel, Houston Texans (ret.)

The book made me both laugh and cry. *Rugged Discipleship* is a fun and thoughtful look at making disciples in the 21st century. It shows us how we can return to Jesus' *rugged* model and principles of discipleship. Steve dives into his personal journey of being discipled by influential and godly men and their profound relationships. As one of the best in leadership development and disciple making in the world of sport, Steve shares how you can reach a new depth of discipleship and be a *rugged* influencer, just as Jesus was/is, in today's world.

Katie Connor, Missionary Midwife Trainer, Haiti

In his new book, *Rugged Discipleship*, Steve Connor captures the essence of the church's most important call—to disciple and embrace Mathew 28. I've watched firsthand Steve grow the next generation of leaders. In his new book, Steve weaves his personal stories with rock solid biblical principles. A must-read for those passionate about impacting lives for eternity.

Cary K. Curry, College Discipleship Ministry, and Author of *An Unlikely Discipler*

I have been blessed to have been discipled by Steve Connor during my time as a college athlete and beyond. For those not as fortunate as I, this book is the next best thing. This book is packed with stories and a wealth of practical wisdom.

Matt Dooley, Pittsburgh Steeler (ret.), Co-owner of The Dooley Collective

Steve Connor has been making disciples for decades. In his newest book, he takes us inside his disciple-making life/process so that we don't just learn *rugged* discipleship, but we experience *rugged* discipleship. You will finish this book feeling encouraged and better prepared to make *rugged* disciples.

D. G. Elmore, Chairman of the Board of Navigators, and Business Entrepreneur

This book was for me! Steve was my ultimate mentor through my college years. I will always cherish the lessons he taught me, and the love his family showed me. From a *rugged* football player to a *rugged* molder of young men, Steve is the best! Read the book and feel the love!

Wes Martin, Washington Redskins

Steve Connor has written a must-read for anyone considering ministry as his life pursuit. ... Read this book, *Rugged Discipleship*—and learn from the best."

Rev. Joseph C Spears Jr., Ed.D, Professor at Bowie State University and Liberty University

Steve's new book reminds me of our time together! Steve has been such an example of God's love throughout the years. He has blessed my life and will undoubtedly bless many others through his dedication of sharing God's Word in sports ministry and beyond. I will always carry fond memories of Steve and his wife, Michelle, opening up their home to myself and fellow IU players. It always felt like "home" while enjoying some added perks of zip lining, four-wheelers, and Michelle's home cooking! From being my Indiana University football chaplain, to preparing my (now) wife and me for marriage, I am so grateful to know him.

Jason Spriggs, Green Bay Packers

What a great read: it brings me back to my time with the Connors. I am very thankful to have had Steve and his wife Michelle teach us and open their doors for us during our formative college years. They always made us feel at home, and really encouraged us to live for Jesus. Read it and get *rugged*!

Nate Sudfeld, Philadelphia Eagles

I have known Steve Connor for well over three decades and regard him as a leader of leaders, a discipler par excellence, an inspirational preacher, thoughtful writer, mentor to many around the globe and a dear friend. I relish Steve's passion for ministry. He truly brings out the best in others and has been instrumental in growing leaders in the most unlikely places. I treasure his friendship and celebrate our partnership in the gospel. His newest book grabs one's attention from the first line of the introduction (the part many readers skip.) Steve lives ruggedly for the Lord. What's more, he has spent his adult life doing exactly what he presents in his latest book. This is good stuff for those who are serious about serving Jesus Christ.

Tom Ellsworth, Senior Pastor, Sherwood Oaks

Foreword

If you are like me, you may want to know what gives this book credence. I think I can answer that question for you and give you some perspective. I have been involved in Sports Ministry to one degree or another: as an athlete, a coach, a professor of sports ministry courses, and as a participant in sports ministry projects and outreaches.

Connor's book *Rugged Discipleship* is a unique, fun, and motivating fusion of Biblical principles, adventure literature, and travelogue, while always encouraging the reader to be and make *rugged* disciples. The writer introduces us to the North Georgia mountains, a wee village in Scotland, jumping trains to Canada, adventures in India, and mysterious friends in Cambodia—from wild skydivers, Chicago Bears, and a motorcycle stolen in Bulgaria.

I have been involved in ministry to one degree or another: as an athlete, a coach, pastor, a professor, and as a participant in global ministry projects and outreaches. In my 50 years of these kinds of activities, I know of no one in the world more competent in Sports Ministry than Dr. Steve Connor. I have watched firsthand his days with the Chicago Bears as he signed his autograph with a Scriptural reference so kids could go to the Bible and make ongoing discoveries about God's love for them. I watched in those days as he used the limelight he enjoyed speaking to various audiences, always pointing people to Jesus. His professional days are in the past, but he made the most of those days, and the effect of his witness during that time continues. I watched him employ his entrepreneurial skill in developing a ministry called "Night of Champions" in which tens of thousands of young men and women came to faith over several decades. I watched as he started a ministry, from scratch, in Great Britain, which is now one of the most extensive parachurch youth ministries in the UK, in part because of his effective partnership with churches. He conceived of this ministry, developed its strategies, and trained and developed other people to work with him and eventually replace him, thereby handing the department off to the Brits. He enjoys seeing its long-term success beyond the fifteen years he invested in the UK.

During those days, I saw him preach before the future King of England. The Archbishop of Canterbury at the time, George Carey, has used and endorsed his youth initiatives. The Scriptures remind us that when a man does his work well, he will stand before kings (Proverbs 22:29); this has certainly been true of Steve. He has worked efficiently with professional athletes, college athletes (as a chaplain), with high school, junior high school, and youth programs, and adult programs, all with significant effect.

I have had the privilege of co-teaching Sports Ministry courses with Steve. I have seen, in one instance, how his instruction was applied by some of his students in setting up a sports ministry at a juvenile detention center where over 600 kids came to faith over a six-year period. I am aware of ministries he has fostered, built, and encouraged in England, Scotland, Wales, Poland, Portugal, Corsica, and Cambodia, as well as in several countries in the Middle East, Latin America, and in states across America. Furthermore, Steve has taken what he has learned, and made it accessible to thousands through the ten books he has written. I had the joy of sitting in the crowd as his alma mater bestowed upon him an honorary doctorate duly awarded to honor his years of faithful service. Steve casts a wide wake. Many will be in heaven because of his life and influence for Christ.

Furthermore, he has trained and discipled thousands of others how to make disciples, in urban, rural, suburban environments, in large population centers, and isolated developing world contexts. He is a remarkably gifted man, one of the most gifted I have ever met. He gives of his time, his energy, his resources, and in his books: his insight and wisdom gained over many years of faithful service, across a wide variety of situations and circumstances. I highly recommend Steve's expertise generally to anyone (pastors, youth workers, lay workers, etc.) wanting to serve Christ by "reproducing reproducers," and I recommend his insights specifically to those with a heart for Sports Ministry.

Steve has now produced *Rugged Discipleship: Show Me Your Friends, I Will Show You Your Future*. The book is not merely a book about disciple-making, it is a telling of Steve's story. It also opens the door for each of us, in whatever occupation, to understand our own stories better. It celebrates context: who we are in Christ, how our lives have been shaped by those who came before us, and the significant part each of us can play in the lives of those we find following behind us. The book is not merely a set of propositions: the transfer of information, mind to mind. *Rugged Discipleship* is filled with stories that put flesh on the bones. These are real-life stories that grow out of the wealth of experiences the author has had. Each story reveals something Dr. Connor has learned through failures and successes in the context of working with people. The lessons learned have something of the radiance of divine leading and purpose shining through. Here is practical wisdom that cannot be found better stated anywhere else. I highly recommend this book. As you read it, you may want to kick your shoes off, for you are entering Holy Ground!

Dr. Jerry Root, Professor of Evangelism, Wheaton College, and Director of the Evangelism Initiative, Billy Graham Center for Evangelism

Acknowledgments

To the Source of every good thing, praise and gratitude to God, our Father. Thank you so much to my wife Michelle, who will stop on a dime and listen with gentle critique and encouragement to every idea I have, both the goofy and good. To Greg Linville for his *rugged* support and oversight to turn an idea into a reality. For the excellent direction of Crin and Brad Pullins, to pull clarity out of a fog. To Scott Simpson, my Australian editor-and-chief and *rugged* encourager. To my *rugged* friends Mel Arnold, Jeff Canada, Phil Mann, Tony Roberto (my dress and music guide), Bob Vansetten, Dan Stevens (Dr. Ming), you are massive influencers in my life (I need to write "part two"). To my rugby coach and Scottish technical advisor Andy Yeaman, a huge thanks! Thank you for the Kingdom's heart and loving service of Stan Terhune, for your encouragement and refinement. I am grateful for the many hundreds of partners I have trained and labored alongside in God's Kingdom.

Finally, I am grateful to you, the readers. Thank you for making *rugged* disciples.

*All proceeds from this book go to world missions.

Introduction

Discipleship is: "Not a program."[1]
"Show me your friends, I will show you your future."[2]
"'Abraham believed God, and it was counted to him as righteousness'—and he was called a friend of God."[3]

Where are they now?

Sometimes the best way to disciple someone is to ask a lot of questions and listen. I think a guy called Socrates may have agreed with me. What do you think?

A former linebacker, Oye, from Nigerian ancestry, was staying at our home. He is an articulate and discerning Christian. Oye was staying with us while he wrestled over whether to leave his business job and go into full-time ministry back at the university where he attended and played football. We spent time together sailing, goofing around with my kids, and having excellent Bible study and discussions.

I asked Oye, "So, what is keeping you from full-time ministry?" Oye said, "Too many of my friends who came to my college Bible study are so far from living a Christian life." Oye went on, "College ministry is great but, *where are they now?*"

We discussed the Parable of the Sower.[4] We observed that too many believers have wilted in the face of adversity. Oye was concerned for so many young Christians who were seemingly unprepared, as Western culture becomes more secularized. We both

noticed that many of the college students we encouraged were being choked out by materialism and false idols. We lamented that there was a lack of theological depth in many churches and organizations. We both agreed that Christians were

---

[1] Bill Hull, *The Complete Book of Discipleship: On Being and Making Followers of Christ*, pp. 295-296. The most common mistake made by well-intentioned leaders, particularly acute in the Global North, is turning discipleship into a curriculum that a serious disciple completes and then graduates from.
[2] Maurice Clarett, a signature phrase used by him to explain both positive and negative influences that will affect your life.
[3] James 3:23.
[4] Matthew 13:1-23; Mark 4:1-20; Luke 8:4-15.

not equipped for the wave of subtle and not-so-subtle persecution that they will undoubtedly face.

Our conversation was starting to get cynical. It is easy to get sophomoric and merely pontificate on all the problems there are with the church. Remember, the church is the Bride of Christ, and is amazingly beautiful. Perfect? No. Adored by Jesus? Yes! I wanted to turn this conversation around and look at solutions. Eventually, I asked Oye, "So what is the answer?" He fired back, "We need more *rugged* Christians!" I asked, "How do we grow *rugged* Christians?" He blurted out, "Rugged discipleship." That phrase has stuck with me for years. To grow *rugged* Christians who will face adversity with courage, they need *rugged* disciple makers.

Let me introduce you to a few.

Chapter 1
Rugged Ingredients: Principles for Rugged Action

"His concern was not with programs to reach the multitudes, but with men whom the multitudes would follow."[5] As my family sat down to a great meal, lovingly (and seemingly effortlessly) prepared by my wife Michelle, we heard the familiar ping that signaled a text message. Instinctively, we all sheepishly pulled our phones out of our pockets to see who had broken the family rule and left his ringer on during dinner. My frown was quickly replaced by embarrassment when I realized it was mine. I raised my hand "mea-culpa-style" and said: "Oops! Sorry, guys, it was me!" My son quickly frowned and raised his eyebrows with an exaggerated look of mock disapproval; it was a good impression of how I must look when someone else forgets to turn his phone off at dinner. It is so much fun to tease Dad!

The text, as it turns out, was from Jake, one of the fastest collegiate athletes on the planet, a young man I had been discipling for over a year. It read: "Steve, I'm going crazy. Can we talk?" The text didn't surprise me. I had noticed that his expressions on various social media platforms (usually upbeat and funny) had recently become somewhat vague and indifferent. After dinner, I excused myself and replied to the text: "Let's meet at the stadium in an hour." I bet the apostle Paul would have loved smartphones!

While traveling to the stadium, my mind cycled through a list of what emergencies Jake might be going through. Over the years, I have heard a lot of these emergencies from young men that I have discipled: "Steve, my girlfriend is pregnant." "Steve, I don't think I am a Christian anymore." "Hey man, I got drunk and was arrested." "Yo, Rev, I don't think God will forgive me. What do you think?" "Steve, my father, has died." "Steve, I am not in love with my spouse anymore." "Hey, chaplain, come over to my dorm. I want you to tell my roommate about Jesus. . ."

---

[5] Robert Coleman, Master Plan of Evangelism.

3

I couldn't help but think how much Jake reminded me of myself (except for the world-class speed part!). I recognized that though his faith was currently fragile, he had incredible potential for leadership. Jake was a young believer and struggled with a few inconsistencies. His life had the usual college-athlete cacophonies with all the frenzied ups-and-downs that come with the stress of competition and collegiate temptations. Oh, my: he also had a keen interest in the ladies. What made Jake so remarkable was his passion for learning, and a hunger to see his teammates become *rugged* Christians.

Tonight, Jake needed a little guidance and a lot of encouragement. As I drove to the stadium, in the rain, I recalled and thanked God for all the remarkable people that have courageously discipled, reassured, and encouraged me over the years. I parked the car in the nearly vacant lot, prayed a quick prayer for guidance, and walked to the stadium.

Jake and I talked for an hour, or should I say he spoke, and I mainly listened and asked a few helpful questions along the way (Jesus loved to ask questions)! I think I provided a little reassurance. We read from the Bible, and we prayed.

Then I did what Jesus often did with His disciples. I asked Jake if he wanted to come over for dinner the next night. (Have I mentioned anything about my wife's delicious cooking?) Jesus' disciples seemed always to enjoy dining together, and what college kid doesn't need a free meal?

One thing I love about making disciples is that no two days are ever the same! The disciple-making process is challenging, often because it is so varied. There's no "cookie-cutter" recipe, and no two people have the exact same journey to spiritual maturity.

> There's no "cookie-cutter" recipe, and no two people have the exact same journey to spiritual maturity.

I wish the Apostle Paul, or any of the Gospel writers, had created a singular "How to" chapter in the Bible to take us through a linear, step-by-step progression of the disciple-making process. They didn't. However, if we observe Jesus and His disciples carefully, we can draw out timeless ingredients (principles), and learn how to recreate the process for our 21st-century disciples.

4

Jesus was a man of action, and His method was not like a professor who merely expostulates various theories. Jesus made disciple-makers who made disciple-makers, and His model was to be obeyed by every follower that came after Him. The time the Apostles spent with Jesus was *rugged* and challenging. Jesus also set the highest standard (a sinless life), and then lived it out before their eyes. The Apostle Paul boldly said, "Be imitators of me, as I am of Christ."[6] and even though we are sinners, we are nevertheless challenged to obediently follow in His footsteps.

We are to strive to do our best to employ Jesus' key strategy for the redemption of the world. What was that plan? *Rugged* relational discipleship. This is what this book is about: taking our Lord's model of *rugged* words (eternal truth) and *rugged* deeds and turning them into *rugged* action for a new generation of *rugged* people.

The life God calls us to is full of adversity. Yet, God made us for significant challenges, and when we respond in obedience, we feel His pleasure and enjoy His grand purpose. *"Everyone then who hears these words of mine and does them will be like a wise man who built his house on the rock."*[7]

Jake did, in fact, come over for dinner the next night. I was amazed at how fast his emergencies (which seemed earth-shattering the night before) were reconciled and forgotten. A new dilemma was brewing, and I was glad to be there for him.

POSTSCRIPT:

Interacting in the chaos of a human's life and helping him to know God and become a *rugged* follower of Jesus Christ, is long, hard, and *rugged* work. Making disciple-makers that, in turn, make disciple-makers (to reproduce reproducers) may be the most challenging, and at times, the most frustrating thing you may ever tackle. (I know the men and women who discipled me were indeed—at times—frustrated with me.) But making disciple-makers who in turn make disciple-makers can also be

---

[6] 1 Corinthians 11:1.
[7] Matthew 7:24.

the most rewarding pursuit of your life. The Great Commission[8] can be intimidating, but it becomes less daunting when we better understand Jesus' strategy. Taking a close examination of Jesus' life, we can discover some of the ingredients that He employed to train His disciples; it will give us clarity.

Have you noticed that some of the best students, athletes, and artists are rarely the best teachers or coaches? One reason is that their performance has become so intuitive, they find it hard to break down and explain the fundamentals of the subject they wish to teach.

> *If I asked you, "What are the ingredients that Jesus used in making disciples?" could you tell me?*

If I asked you: "What are the ingredients that Jesus used in making disciples?" could you tell me? If you can't, you are not alone. Many of my colleagues, who are effective disciple-makers, struggle to articulate how they do it. They may offer a few programs or possible steps to spiritual progression, but they have trouble verbalizing the principles Jesus employed to make disciples.

For example, my wife, Michelle, is a master cook. She has enjoyed preparing meals for years, and for so many people, it has become an intuitive skill. She's been cooking so long that she could do it blindfolded—a dash of this, a dollop of that, and one tiny smattering of those produce something beautiful. The problem is that when something becomes intuitive, it can become harder to teach.

Unfortunately, because Michelle's cooking is now so intuitive, she has sometimes found it challenging to explain the process of how she comes up with such a wonderful meal, even to train our children and me to cook! We ask her: "How much exactly is a dash? How much is a dollop? What is a smatter?"

This illustration can be used in many ways: What are the ingredients of a championship team? What are the

---

[8] "Go therefore and make disciples of all nations, baptizing them in the name of the Father and of the Son and of the Holy Spirit, teaching them to observe all that I have commanded you. And behold, I am with you always, to the end of the age." Matthew 28:19, 20.

6

ingredients of your favorite piece of music? What are the principles[9] needed to create a healthy business?

In this book, we will examine both the disciple-making ingredients/principles Jesus used in the training of the Twelve, and we will explore my personal journey to discipleship, both its many failures and successes.

Of course, like any great recipe or masterpiece, Jesus' ingredients of disciple-making blend together. No one component stands alone. It is the fusion of the ingredients that make a healthy product. In each chapter, we will highlight one ingredient that Jesus employed in building His disciples. We will simultaneously be reminding ourselves that discipleship does not happen in a silo. It is the combination of several ingredients working together to create a *rugged* soul.

FOR CONTEMPLATION:

- What timeless principles of disciple-making come to mind as you consider Jesus' methodology?
- In your opinion, what is the most attractive principle or ingredient that Jesus employed?
- What principle do you need to develop?

---

[9] A principle is a central, universal, timeless, and clear truth that serves as the foundation for a system of belief.

Chapter 2
Rugged Infants: More Babies Than Mamas

"But I, brothers, could not address you as spiritual people, but as people of the flesh, as infants in Christ. I fed you with milk, not solid food, for ye were not ready for it..."[10]

"Clearly the policy of Jesus at this point teaches us that whatever method of follow-up the church adopts, it must have at its basis a personal guardian concerned for those entrusted to their care. To do otherwise is essentially to abandon new believers to the devil."[11]

On a wet and chilly English night, Michelle and I were sound asleep only to be startled by the phone ringing. Fighting disorientation, I answered. The voice of the man on the other end of the phone seemed scared and urgent. It was Scott, one of my American football players, a big lineman for the Oxford Saints (United Kingdom). I was Scott's head coach; he was a tough, hard-drinking, fun-loving guy that didn't seem interested in anything to do with Christianity. Michelle and I moved to England to help pioneer sports ministry, and as the coach for Oxford, I introduced a chapel program and a midweek Bible study. Scott had little interest, and playfully mocked my faith. But his banter was good-natured, and I truly loved the man. Tonight, however, Scott sounded austere and frightened.

Scott was living with his girlfriend, Anne. She was beautiful, and I encouraged him to marry her! Anne had gotten pregnant, and to their credit, they did not kill the baby. But the birth was a long way away... or so we thought.

Anne, as I learned from the phone call, had prematurely gone into labor at 27 weeks. This was dangerous, and understandably Scott was scared. Scott was on the phone telling me he was at the John Radcliffe Hospital in Oxford. "Could I

---

[10] 1 Corinthians 3:1, 2.
[11] Robert Coleman, Master Plan of Evangelism.

please come down and pray for his wife and baby?" They named her Ellie!

I dragged myself out of bed and rushed to the hospital. The baby was born. Anne was going to be okay, but baby Ellie was fighting for her precious little life. The odds of her survival were not good. I walked into the SCBU (Special Care Baby Unit) not knowing what to expect. I am comfortable walking into any locker-room in the world, and praying for a high-profile athlete, but this was outside of my comfort zone. I wondered if the doctors, midwives, and nurses would be disapproving of an American football coach coming in the middle of the night to pray for a premature baby. No worries: they were remarkably welcoming.

Now I was trembling. A midwife led me back to the baby incubator. I was startled at how "wee" Ellie was. Gently I stuck my hand into the plastic glove that was built into the machine and touched her perfectly formed hand. She actually seemed to hang on to my finger, which in proportion to her tiny hand looked like she was grasping a log. Through a hesitant and shaky voice, I prayed for Ellie, for her health and growth, for her parents; and I thanked God for the excellent medical team that surrounded her. Praise be to God, Ellie has grown into a beautiful woman, and later I had the privilege of marrying Scott and Anne.

Now don't get me wrong: I certainly don't have the gift of healing, as evidenced by the many men and women that I have prayed for over the years who have died. Nonetheless, I will never forget the night I prayed for Ellie and felt God's peace and power.

> Now don't get me wrong: I certainly don't have the gift of healing, as evidenced by the many men and women that I have prayed for over the years who have died.

In addition to my prayers, the American football team that Scott and I were part of rallied behind the birth. We all talked about Ellie and her mother's recovery. It took a vast amount of time, care, resources, and energy, but Ellie was finally able to go home. We all watched her grow. We all know she is a modern-day miracle.

POSTSCRIPT:

Most people would do whatever it took to nurture a premature baby to safety and health. So why don't we do a better job with a premature Christian?

A fundamental privilege for Christians is to enjoy being in Jesus's presence and be transformed into His likeness. This takes time and resources. Could it be that the Great Commission[12] is not only crucial to the health of the church, but also a key to our own transformation and spiritual maturity? If we are to experience the Christian life fully, it is understandable that we are to follow Jesus' *rugged* example and be obedient to His teachings.

Sadly, so many Christians stay spiritually immature, and they are rarely encouraged to "Go therefore and make disciples."[13] This is tragic because making disciples who will make disciples is key not only to the health of the Body of Christ, but to every individual believer's spiritual maturity. Jesus warned us that there were too many "sheep without a shepherd."[14] He commanded his disciples to, "Therefore pray earnestly to the Lord of the harvest to send out laborers into his harvest."[15]

Jesus Sends Help

Remember, before Jesus ascended to heaven, He promised a "Councilor/Advocate," the "Holy Spirit," to His top guys.[16]

If I were one of Jesus's disciples, I would be scratching my head and wondering what it meant to have a "Jesus councilor." The disciples, who had spent the best of three *rugged* years with Jesus, didn't need some mysterious Holy Spirit. All they had to do was lean in and talk to their Master directly about whatever was on their mind.

Now Jesus was gone! At the beginning of the book of Acts, we find that Jesus was crucified, dead, buried and resurrected. Jesus had appeared to His disciples and many followers; and finally ascended to heaven. We next see the disciples huddled

---

[12] Matthew 28:19.
[13] Matthew 28:19.
[14] Matthew 9:36.
[15] Matthew 9:38.
[16] John 14:6.

10

in fear together in Jerusalem, praying desperately for guidance. This was happening during the Jewish holiday of Pentecost, and the Holy City of Jerusalem was packed with first-century tourists. Everyone in Jerusalem was in a festive mood, and "there were dwelling in Jerusalem Jews, devout men from every nation."[17] The disciples most likely heard the happy hustle and bustle of a huge crowd packed into the festive city outside their rooms. However, Jesus' disciples were not in the mood for a holiday.

I bet the disoriented disciples deeply missed their Friend/ Leader/Master. They must have been doing their very best to fight off bewilderment and fear. Their idea of the future had been shattered with Jesus' crucifixion: perhaps they were asking: "Now what!"

They had no idea what life would be like with their Master gone. All their experiences, challenges and adventures with Jesus, their companionship, late-night talks, formal and informal instruction with their amazing rabbi seemed to have vanished. Little did they know that all their experience and training was part of God's incredible strategy for the redemption of the world. A global spiritual movement was about to explode. Their training was about to be turned into action.

The disciples in all their confusion earnestly kept praying. Just as Jesus had promised, the Holy Spirit, like a champion prizefighter, made a grand entry. The Holy Spirit "suddenly" filled the room like a storm, and while the disciples were praying, they were filled with power.[18] Like Jesus promised, the Spirit arrived, and the world would never be the same.

The diverse crowd at Pentecost in Jerusalem was amazed because these men started speaking to them in their own language. Suddenly Peter, a seemingly new man, was filled with the Spirit, and could not help himself. He was compelled to invite the world to love and follow his Master. The crowd responded to Peter's message: "they were cut to the heart," and the church, "the Bride of Christ," emerged.

What a great problem to have! The Holy Spirit spoke through Peter during the festival, and men and women were moved. Scripture says: "So those who received his word were baptized, and there were

---

[17] Acts 2:5.
[18] Acts 2:1-6.

added that day about three thousand souls."[19] The disciples were at a crossroad: they could either move forward as disciple-makers, or wallow in despair because Jesus was gone. Three thousand souls respond to the gospel, and thankfully, all the training the disciples had received from their Master was about to kick into high gear.

Why did Jesus spend the largest amount of His three-year ministry with a small number of people? Since the day of Pentecost, Jesus' plans to concentrate a significant proportion of His time on the training of the twelve (and several other disciples, men and women) was about to become crystal clear. The first wave of Christians did not

> *The first wave of Christians did not need a program to navigate their faith; they needed guides.*

need a program to navigate their faith; they needed guides. We read in the book of Acts that the disciples had plenty of complications and many lessons still to learn, but the disciples, whether they understood it or not, were equipped to build the church. The disciples were the major actors in God's divine plan: a plan that carries on to this day: a plan that you and I have been part of since the beginning of time.

New Challenges

Since the exciting first days of the emerging church, there has been adversity. Wars, famine, political unrest, false Biblical teachings, and revolutions have shifted the demographics of Christ-followers. Great sanctuaries have fallen; God's people have been martyred and exiled. Wars have destroyed families, communities, and cultures, but disciples of Jesus (God's redemptive strategy) have continued to spread, and at many times flourished in these *rugged* times. Methodology for making disciples has changed over the centuries, but Jesus's plan to build His church through disciple-making is timeless.

Throughout history, we have had the same dilemma of having several young and immature Christians, and only a few brave leaders ("shepherds") to respond to Jesus' Great Commission and nurture the babies to maturity. The Apostle Paul understood this all too well. He seems exasperated when he writes to the Corinthian church, *"But I, brothers, could not*

---

[19] Acts 2:40.

address you as spiritual people, but as people of the flesh, as infants in Christ. "[20]

Perhaps you face the same problem the disciples had after the Pentecost revival: more converts than workers. In other words, the Holy Spirit shows up, and we have way too many babies, and not enough parents to help nurture the children to healthy Christian maturity. There has been a reoccurring historical cycle of spiritual conversion, a vacuum of spiritual depth, and then an imperative for authentic discipleship. In other words, we "out-punt our coverage." Fortunately, many congregations are rediscovering that disciple-making is Jesus's vital strategy for growing *rugged* Christians.

Since the mid-twentieth century, the world has become far more transient. I believe that compared to previous generations, we are experiencing a diminished sense of community. The church also struggles with this problem. When I a look at an old photograph of an adult Sunday school, most of the men and women were born, raised, and died in the same region. For good and bad, congregations experienced a sense of community.

Our great-grandparents consumed a diet that was mainly produced within a one-hundred-mile radius of their home. The world rapidly changed with the advent of the train, automobile and the expansion of roads, airline industry, and social media. Society has changed as our world became easier to travel and communicate. With the advent of the transportation revolution, new opportunities abound. More to the point, it expanded our choices of where to attend church. My daughter is a missionary in Haiti. In a developing world, you may think that church is still community-based. I was surprised as I was preaching one Sunday at how many people were traveling (often by motorcycle taxi) up and down the city to worship at a variety of churches.

When I travel to the remotest areas of Africa, I find shops full of consumables from North America and Europe. Variety seems to be everywhere. Though homegrown produce is a pleasure, most people now take for granted our globalized markets. Markets have become more competitive, and have learned to attract customers, often in crafty ways. Much of the

---

[20] 1 Corinthians 3:1.

human race has become intelligent consumers and expects competition and variety. If global consumers don't like the product they have purchased, they will happily change brand, store, or website.

The church may be one of the last bastions of consumer brand loyalty, as evidenced by a whole generation of people sticking to their church and denomination even though its mission and theology has shifted well off its Biblical foundations. But like many markets in our globalized world, churches have also been challenged with a transient consumer-based populace. Many churches adapted, and many have died.

A healthy church clings to Biblical principles while adapting their practice. Yet, while we adapt, we continually need to be anchored to sound Biblical truth. In the past forty years, a new wave of leaders with an entrepreneurial spirit, and a genuine desire to reach the world for Christ, has developed a new "church growth" methodology. One manifestation of this emphasis has been the emergence of the "mega-church." Sadly, it has become fashionable to bash mega-church pioneers for preaching a shallow gospel. I have known several mega-church leaders, and I can attest that their purest desire was/is to reach as many lost souls as they could in a culturally tumultuous era.

Some of their church-growth methodologies were based on Biblical principles, and yes, some of it was based on a free-market consumer attraction strategy. Yet, mega-churches have reached many people that historical churches would never impact. The fact remains, however, that many of those who were attracted to such congregations remain spiritually shallow and in desperate need of a more vibrant and deeper walk with Christ. I believe the deeper walk is best attained, not by an attraction-based consumer approach to church, but rather through Jesus' model of making disciples!

For good and bad, the church worldwide has been infected with many church growth philosophies and methodologies. This new wave of church expansion has created a new generation who are hungry for *rugged*, authentic spiritual encouragement.

Several churches and para-ministries over the past decade recognize the fact that the church has a "spiritual depth problem," due to a transient community that lacks an understanding of spiritual growth and authentic relationships. Jesus is our

> *Jesus is our Model, yet we have ignored many of His most strategic training principles.*

Model, yet we have ignored many of His most strategic training principles. A renewed interest in Jesus's disciple-making has reemerged, but it is *rugged* work.

Imagine Jesus recruiting the twelve disciples, and saying, "Let us meet once a week at Starbucks for a half hour before you go fishing or tax collecting. We will go through a six-week training course on 'How to Redeem the World.' Then you boys will be ready for the greatest challenge of your life—you will be prepared to fish for men." Imagine that after the six-week-course, Jesus threw them into the work after Pentecost. They would not have succeeded.

FOR CONTEMPLATION:

Granted, a six-week half-hour course on being a disciple of Christ is better than nothing; yet Jesus' model was more *rugged*, personal, and hands-on. Some churches will only provide a Sunday sermon to help you mature spiritually; some churches offer a smorgasbord of programs to "meet your spiritual needs." Other churches claim to provide a "map" to spiritual maturity. But disciples that make disciples provide a guide. Jesus' plan to bring Christians to maturity is costly in time, effort, and occasionally heartbreak. It by necessity will require a *rugged* sacrifice.

- Our commission to prepare disciples to impact the Kingdom of God is as crucial and immediate as it was in the first century. Why (in some cases) does the church not value disciple-making?

- By examining Jesus' process, we learn many of our microwave methods of nurturing Christians are producing shallow and, in some cases, anemic followers of Christ. We would never throw premature babies out of the hospital. We should never do it with young Christians either. How do we create a *rugged* culture of disciple-making?

Chapter 3
Rugged Reminder: Rocks and Men

"Take care lest you forget the LORD your God by not keeping his commandments and his rule and his statutes, which I command you today, ... then your heart be lifted up, and you forget the LORD your God, who brought you out of the land of Egypt, out of the house of slavery...'"[21]

"When all the nation had finished passing over the Jordan, the LORD said to Joshua, 'Take twelve men from the people, from each tribe a man, and command them, saying, "Take twelve stones from here out of the midst of the Jordan, from the very place where the priests' feet stood firmly, and bring them over with you and lay them down in the place where you lodge tonight." [He did that] 'so that all the peoples of the earth may know that the hand of the LORD is mighty, that you may fear the LORD your God forever.'"[22]

A Rugged Reminder

Humans have a tendency to forget about God. We need *rugged* reminder. What certain aromas or sounds bring you back to

your childhood? I find it interesting that sounds or smells can be a bridge to lost memories. The scent of logs burning in a fireplace reminds me of campouts that I have not thought of in years. Walking on grass after it's first cut in the spring reminds me of football practice. And the sound of rain pattering on a windowpane on a wet winter night brings me back to one low spot in my life when God gave me a sucker-punch in the gut, and said: "Hey punk, stop feeling sorry for yourself. You are pitiful. Don't you remember all the amazing people I put in your life?"

I have read that God is patient, but on this night, He was quick to capture my attention. After a few fun games and prayers, I had put the kids to bed while my wife, Michelle,

---

[21] Deuteronomy 8:11, 14.
[22] Joshua 4:1-3, 24.

was enjoying her "Ladies' Book Club" in our small, quirky village in the southern highlands of Scotland. She had joined the club because she loved the women in our community, and wanted to get to know them better. Some of the books they read were interesting, while some were dark and disturbing. We both loved our community, and Michelle hoped she could introduce some books and conversations that would lead them to more spiritual discussions and feed their souls.

It was late when she arrived home, and the rain was gently bouncing off the windowpane of our 150-year-old stone-built Scottish house. She quietly changed and then slipped into bed. "How did it go?" I asked her. I usually gleaned something interesting from the literature the women read and discussed. Moreover, I learned a bit more about the spiritual climate in our village, as many of these ladies' partners or spouses were also my friends.

I asked her, in a curious but underlying sanctimonious tone: "Did you have an opportunity to share your faith?" "No," came Michelle's reply, "but I did share my love. There was no real appropriate time to talk about Christ overtly. We were talking about our new book, which dealt with cooking." I was somewhat annoyed with her. I guess it is because so many Christians I know seem ashamed of having a conversation about Jesus with their non-Christian friends: that is, if they have any non-Christian friends at all.

To my shame, my attitude was self-righteous. Sharing my faith, over time, had come relatively easily to me. I expected Michelle to be the same. Then the ugly curse of self-pity took hold, and I said to myself: "Why is Michelle so reluctant to share her faith? She has had such an easy life! After all, I was the product of a dysfunctional household. My parents divorced when I was young; my mother suffered from schizophrenia. My father was an alcoholic, had lived a wild skydiving lifestyle, and was killed when I was 20. I have had it hard, and my wife has had it easy! She had the incredible luxury of having a nuclear family. They may have never talked about faith or feelings in the home, but at least she had a home!"

I don't think I could have identified the destructive emotions coursing through me: a strange mixture of self-pity and self-righteousness (a toxic combination for anyone, but especially lethal for a guy in ministry).

> I don't think I could have identified the destructive emotions coursing through me: a strange mixture of self-pity and self-righteousness (a toxic combination for anyone, but especially lethal for a guy in ministry).

While the rain was beating on the windows, I looked out at the ancient graveyard across the street. It was then God lost patience with me and decided to get my attention. He punched me right in the gut! It's not often that I get these not-so-subtle spiritual epiphanies (if I did, I would always look like I was on the losing end of an MMA fight), but this felt as close to a real punch as I've ever had from the Supernatural.

I felt my gut contract, and an almost audible voice came to me and said: "Will you stop feeling sorry for yourself! I sent you the most amazing spiritual nurturing people a man could have. I gave you Coach Rex, Jack, Jerry, Terry and an unbelievable host of Ateam friends that lifted you right out of hell. You have had an incredible team of Christian leaders in your life, and I have given you a beautiful wife and family. I gave you an incredible education and life experiences. How dare you have a pity party!"

Michelle was a bit surprised when I explained to her what had just happened. With misty eyes, I asked her to forgive me. And then, as we do every night, we prayed together. We prayed for our friends in our beautiful village, and I asked God to forgive me for being a jerk. He did. I have asked Him to forgive me often.

After our prayer, Michelle drifted off to sleep. I, however, was wakeful. I started to recall all those relationships that have intersected my life and influenced my spiritual pilgrimage—all those living memorials that have reminded me about an incredible adventure with my Holy Father.

As I considered all the fantastic people that God put in my path, His (not-so-subtle) reminder made me more ashamed of the self-righteous feelings and pity that had come over me that night. When I look back at how our Lord has loved me—a chubby, insecure kid—through so many men and women, I am deeply grateful.

Have you ever had one of those encounters with God? A reminder of His love for you, and the blessings He has bestowed on you? I think He speaks to us more than we realize.

God continues to reveal Himself; He has reminded me of His love for at-risk kids through a rainbow arching over a small community in Africa. He reminds me of His intimacy as I read the Bible and pray. God confirms His majesty as I ride my motorcycle through a forest on warm autumn afternoons. God has reminded me of His sovereignty while praying for my young son's fever to break.

God continues to reach out to us and reveal His incredible power and love. Sadly, because of our hectic lives, we seem to forget those special moments.

God also chooses to reveal Himself and feed our souls through people; especially when we are too young, too stubborn, too unfamiliar, or too blinded to feed ourselves. God has chosen to use humans to play a part in His *rugged* plan for redemption and restoration.

God is at work. He asks His children to be a *rugged* memorial, to stand tall and help direct others to Him. God is reminding us of His glory and desire to transform us from our sinful, broken ways. He is using people like you and me as the paint and brush strokes to restore us to His likeness.

Mysteriously, your part in making disciples will also contribute to your *rugged* restoration. We have a part to play in changing the world. Have you humbly asked God to use you to participate in His redemptive and transformative work? Have you asked God to give you the wisdom to disciple others? Seek out men and women that are mastering the art of disciple-making. Give your life over to helping others to love God more, know Him better, and put into practice an experience utterly committed to God. Get out in the river and pick up a stone.

POSTSCRIPT:

We seem to have short memories.

We humans throughout history have had one thing in common: we tend to forget about God.

19

"You were unmindful of the Rock that bore you, and you forgot the God who gave you birth."[23]

"And the people of Israel did what was evil in the sight of the LORD. They forgot the LORD their God and served the Baals and the Asheroth."[24]

"But they soon forgot his works; they did not wait for his counsel."[25]

You would think that after the Israelites' 40-year camp-out in the desert, where God provided all their needs, they would never forget that epic day when God finally allowed them to cross into the Promised Land. God knows we tend to forget about Him. So, God gave the Israelites a useful reminder. He commanded Joshua (Moses' supernumerary successor) to choose 12 men, one from each tribe.[26] Each of these men was to select a stone from the Jordan River. They were to stack them together in a mound as a memorial. The root word of "memorial" is "memory," a reminder. This mound on the Jordan River was a device to help the Israelites recall God's faithfulness, power, commandments, and redemptive purposes. The Bible tells us that the mound lasted as a memorial to God throughout Joshua's lifetime.

Centuries later, what is Jesus' strategy to fulfill His most essential movement (commission) on the planet? Jesus seemed to have the same challenge Joshua had: a stiff-necked people who had a propensity for forgetting God. How does Jesus go about changing the world? Jesus did not use 12 stones; instead, He used 12 men. He trained 12 specific men, to remind the rest of the world about God. Jesus has been using disciples to tell the world about God ever since.

---

[23] Deuteronomy 32:18.
[24] Judges 3:7.
[25] Psalm 106:13.
[26] Joshua 4:1.

Imagine you were to be chosen by Joshua to represent one of the 12 tribes of Israel! Your job was to lift a stone out of the riverbed of the Jordan River, and erect a memorial. What an honor!

> *Imagine you were to be chosen by Joshua to represent one of the 12 tribes of Israel!*

What a responsibility! Which stone do you pick? How big a stone can you carry? What a joy to be selected for such a noble task! For the rest of your life, your children and grandchildren would regale their friends with the story of how Joshua picked you to help build that an incredible memorial to God.

Imagine the warm smile and sense of satisfaction you have every time you see that great memorial and remember the privilege you had to participate in helping build the monument. The great news is that God has picked you to continue building a memorial— a living monument that continues to bring glory to God.

We have the opportunity to be part of God's story by making disciples, a living memorial—souls fulfilling their purpose by worshiping their Creator. The apostle Paul told the Thessalonian church, *"For what is our hope or joy or crown of boasting before our Lord Jesus at his coming? Is it not you? For you are our glory and joy."* Like Paul, our memorial is not built from a rock, but of men. Imagine the warm smile and sense of satisfaction you have every time you see young men and women living healthy Christian lives! What a privilege that God has chosen you to participate in helping build His monument. As a disciple-maker, I find that "reminding" my disciples is easy and vital.

FOR CONTEMPLATION:

I often ask my disciples a few simple little questions to help kindle self-examination:
- What is God doing in your life lately?
- How can you honor your spouse in a special way today?
- What is a reoccurring sin that keeps defeating you and what are you doing about it?

21

I love to pray for my guys, but I need a good list, or I will forget. Often after my prayers for a specific disciple, I will nudge him with a quick text. For instance, "Hey Dimitric, God told me to remind you that He loves to spend time with you!"

- I used to think I would never forget God, but now I realize I need several *rugged* reminders to remain vibrant in my Christian life.
- Making time to allow God to speak into your life is as vital as a branch staying connected to a vine. Are you staying connected? Jesus said, *"I am the vine, you are the branches. Whoever abides in me and I in him, he it is that bears much fruit, for apart from me you can do nothing."*[27]
- Who were those special people who played an influential role to encourage and remind you to abide in Christ?
- Whom are you helping to "abide," and what steps of can you take to strengthen them today?
- Maybe you need to text them right now and give them a gentle reminder.

---

[27] John 15:5.

Chapter 4
Rugged Longing: Emptiness in the Heart

"You have made us for Yourself, and our hearts are restless until they find their rest in Thee."[28]

"There is a God-shaped vacuum in the heart of every man, and only God can fill it."[29]

"I have seen the business that God has given to the children of man to be busy with. He has made everything beautiful in its time. Also, he has put eternity into man's heart..."[30]

The Germans call it "Sehnsucht," Aristotle called it "desire," Augustine called it a "restless heart," C. S. Lewis called it "longing," and our mid-century philosopher and singer Mick Jager called it "no satisfaction." The advertising boys on Madison Avenue call it "money." King Solomon, who dabbled in the desires of almost everything this world has to offer, and still seemed dissatisfied, said, *"He has put eternity into man's heart."*[31]

Longing Awakens

On reflection, I realized that my discipleship journey started in a hot and sticky field as the sweet-scented corn was at its zenith early one Saturday morning. The insects were just becoming active and were buzzing, but all I could hear was the wheezing from my asthmatic lungs, and the slapping of the sharp green blades, which stretched lazily from their stalk, and clung to my tears, and tore at my cheeks. I was running like a drunken sailor through the furrows for help against hope. My mind was racing. I wasn't certain but was reasonably sure that I had just watched a man die.

---

[28] Augustine of Hippo, *Confessions.*
[29] Blaise Pascal, *Pensées.*
[30] Ecclesiastes 3:10, 11.
[31] Ecclesiastes 3:11.

He was a friend. Not someone I was really close to, or even paid much attention to, but someone I liked all the same. His name was "Twink," I think because he loved Twinkies. I don't know much about him. He seemed kind and gentle; he had a nice young family. I had stayed at his house once, but all I can remember is looking at the strange covers of some Led Zeppelin albums that were scattered around his well-worn stereo system.

As I ran, my stomach retched. I vomited on my shirt, leaving me with a feeling of embarrassment, or weakness, or both. I felt a sense of guilt for being more concerned with the vomit on my shirt than for Twink. Tears distorted my vision, which did not help my already confused equilibrium, and I fell again. In a panic to get help, I ran straight over some tall, rough stalks of corn, and worried that some farmer was going to yell at me.

We have all watched people in the movies cry out for help. This was my turn, but my lungs were gasping for breath, and the words coming out of my mouth sounded foreign, disingenuous, as I tried to scream. I hoped my assessment was wrong and wondered that "perhaps my effort could save his life." I had been wrong before, assuming I had witnessed a fatality when I had not, so I pushed on through the furrows of corn for help. I was twelve.

A few months earlier, I had watched what I thought was my father die in a skydiving accident. He loved skydiving and being around all those adrenalin junkies who lived for risk. Subsequently, I had spent much of my life at rural airports and drop-zones, watching men and women fling themselves out of airplanes. I would happily suspend play in the barns and fields around the airport with other sons and daughters of skydivers (jump-brats) to watch him jump, usually from an old eight-seat Twin Beech.

Dad's specific discipline was known as "FS" or Formation Skydiving. While in free-fall, he would attempt to turn in any direction (any direction but up!) while creating a sequence of formations and maneuvers with other jumpers.

On this occasion, I lay on the grass, listened to the old Twin Beech cut the power of its engine, and watched the jumpers

24

tumble out of the plane. Their formation wasn't tight, but I was sure they were having fun. I couldn't wait until I was old enough to make my first jump.

The skydiving team finally "ran outta sky." They turned away from their formation, and sequentially opened their parachutes. I noticed that one of the skydivers had a malfunction—his main chute was deployed but had not fully opened. To everybody's horror, the person panicked.

Standard procedure (taught to every novice) is to release (cut away) the malfunctioned canopy first, before deploying the reserve (emergency) parachute. Unfortunately, the skydiver made the potentially deadly mistake of panicking, and opened his reserve parachute right into the wad that was his main chute. The skydiver plummeted to the ground; there was no full canopy to break his fall.

I immediately did an inventory, confident that this rookie mistake belonged to someone other than my dad. Skydivers can be an odd bunch. I had been taught to have contempt for those that panicked in the air. I quickly scanned the sky for my father's distinctive blue and white chute that he called "The Blue Max." I could not find it, and my blood went cold as I watched the jumper in the malfunctioned chute hit the ground a half-mile away. Filled with terror, I ran towards the accident.

When emergencies happen, it is interesting to see which skydivers turn and run to help, and which don't. Several of those who were on the ground waiting for their "ride" ran towards the stricken skydiver. but some, surprisingly, didn't. My father always seemed to be the first on the scene, ready to help in an emergency.

Fearfully, I ran to the accident, frightened that I would find my father killed in the accident, wondering why I had not been able to see "The Blue Max" in the sky. Like magic, Dad seemed to appear from nowhere (it still feels mysterious to this day). and tackled me. I learned later that he was jumping with a different parachute that I hadn't recognized. He had landed close to the site of the accident, and seeing me running, stopped me before he carried on to the victim. Dad told me to stay put. He didn't want me to witness what would undoubtedly have been an ugly scene. Then he went to the jumper's aid. I crept closer, probably more out of curiosity than a desire to help. Sadly, I had seen skydivers before, huddled around a casualty with nothing to offer but condolences.

Sensing I was near, my dad, who was a respected skydiving coach as well as an accomplished jumper (he had once set a record for the most jumps in a day by a man over 40), turned my way with a tear in his eye and a gentle smile that looked strangely like relief. He explained to me:

"Everything is going to be okay. The jumper who had panicked was 'Crazy Alice'!"

A mere 18-year-old waif, Alice had been "lucky," saved by a last-second, partial opening of her canopy while hitting a muddy bog from the previous night's downpour. She should have been dead but recovered from a broken ankle to later make a few more skittish jumps before sensibly disappearing from the strange family of adrenalin junkies.

Twink, however, was not so fortunate. His "luck" was out, and I was running on a fool's errand. Twink was part of a team doing formations. He, like "Crazy Alice," also had a malfunction on opening, but instead of a quick "cutaway," he tried to work the canopy open by hand. In doing so, he wasted precious time, and when he finally released the failed chute and went for his "reserve chute," he had "run outta sky," and Twink vanished with a sickening thud into the fields of high corn.

Earlier that morning, I had awakened feeling rather stiff after sleeping on a stack of old parachutes. I was playing by myself near the cornfields, bored and waiting for my friend to arrive, the son of another experienced skydiver.

I had stopped my hike through the corn to watch the skydivers finish their maneuvers and open their chutes. My awe turned to horror as I watched Twink fight to open his parachute, and then disappear into the corn near where I was playing. I was not the first on the scene—two other jumpers had landed close by in an attempt to rescue him. They found Twink after a quick search. It was a bloody, twisted sight, and I was sent to get help. I ran as fast as I could.

It became a long, horrible day as people walked around like zombies, trying to reconcile a life gone. I remember watching my father leave the airport for the grim task of telling

Twink's spouse and two small children the dark news that their husband and father had died.

Perhaps running through the furrows of corn was the start of my pilgrimage—a journey that helped me understand that I was a steward, and not an owner, of the possessions inside this envelope of skin called a human being. Seeing Twink's broken, motionless body, I had to wrestle with the fact that his spirit was gone; if indeed he had a spirit... The thought passed through my mind, if ever so briefly, and I asked myself: "Surely Twink was more than a shattered sack of flesh? If he had a soul, or was, in essence, a soul, where did he go, and to whom did it belong if he belonged to anyone but himself? Was he answerable to some higher power, or was he merely adrift in a spirit world?"

Being a product of the late-20th century, and far from any religious affiliation, the seeds of modernity were well sown into my heart. Even at 12, I clung to the lie that I was an autonomous, self-determinant power. Almost every influence in my young life implied that I was merely a sack of biology, a product of chance through a convoluted evolutionary process. If I was going to worship anything, it was going to be my own life.

> *Being a product of the late-20th century, and far from any religious affiliation, the seeds of modernity were well sown into my heart.*

I was under the spell that I could establish my own moral law and determine the value I placed on my fellow human beings. Twink's death cruelly brought me to a crossroad. If nothing else, it reminded me that we all serve something—at the very least the laws of nature, especially the law of gravity.

Of course, at age 12, I did not think in terms of "autonomy" or of being a "self-determinant human being." Nevertheless, the desire to "do it my way" permeated my young paradigm. Like many other kids, I wanted to lean over the bow of the *Titanic*, spread out my arms, and, like Jack from the 1997 movie about the doomed passenger ship, yell out, "I'm the king of the world."

Yet something was gnawing away inside my calloused heart, which had been peeled back by Twink's death. The question haunted me: "Is this it: live for a little while, and die? Was there more? Was there some power/order (law), and if so, what was that power up to?" I certainly did not want to serve some ambiguous god, or gods, and be obliged to follow their laws.

These questions came like the slow waves of pain—like the beginning of a toothache. One haunting feeling possessed me, and I kept thinking and asking: "Is this all there is, and then you die? What futility! Was there any true meaning in a human's life?"

I felt as if there was a song needing to be played, but it was embedded deep down in my heart, and I needed help to find it. The words of Augustine are most descriptive of my young pilgrimage: *"You have made us for Yourself, and our hearts are restless until they find their rest in Thee."* I was restless.

I still have dreams about Twink's death. I dream I am running through the corn, looking for truth. If it wasn't for an old coach with an an-old-fashioned haircut, I could still be running.

POSTSCRIPT:

I used to think I could never fill the "restless," unfulfilled emptiness in my heart because nothing really permanently satisfied. Life without Jesus is like drinking saltwater: it just makes you thirstier. But now I understand that allowing God to spiritually reside in me, and allowing Him to reign as King, can satisfy the gnawing emptiness. The more I worship God, the more satisfied I become.

We Were Designed to Worship

The Apostle Paul tells us to *"Present your bodies as a living sacrifice, holy and acceptable to God, which is your spiritual act of worship."*[32] Deep in the human soul is an insatiable capacity for worship. If you don't believe me, let me take you to a championship-deciding sporting event to watch fans scream and shout. Though that impulse for worship is often misplaced, we were designed to worship our Creator; we do it with our mind, body, and spirit.

> It may be easier than we think to find common ground as we start to make disciples and help people to worship.

---

[32] Romans 12:1.

There are more than seven billion distinctively made human beings on the planet, yet I find it interesting that most are hardwired with the same central purpose: the desire to worship something, which I believe is *"eternity into man's heart."*[33] It may be easier than we think to find common ground as we start to make disciples and help people to worship.

No two disciples will be the same, but the core foundational principles never change. For example, music has always varied from different cultures and throughout history, but the core foundational elements are still the same: pitch, rhythm, and dynamics. From these core elements come a near-infinite number of musical variations. Learn the core ingredients of discipleship, and you will have a near-infinite variety of ways to disciple others.

To disciple, and be a disciple, is to enjoy the freedom and creativity of expression, as well as to thrive within the boundaries of our eternal design because we are designed to worship God, to know Him, and to serve Him. We want to help people to love God, to worship Him with reckless abandon, to know Him more deeply, and to serve Him. Somehow, we, as followers of Jesus, have forgotten our purpose.

Longing

Ecclesiastes, the enigmatic book of the Bible penned by Solomon, is infused with a feeling of emptiness. Or to quote the author, *"all is vanity."*

King Solomon was famous for his wisdom, wealth, and administrative shrewdness. He built his father's (King David's) kingdom into an unrivaled empire. But in the book of Ecclesiastes, we find that many of the pursuits of man do not satisfy. As C. S. Lewis famously wrote: *"If we find ourselves with a desire that nothing in this world can satisfy, the most probable explanation is that we were made for another world."*

At the end of Ecclesiastes, after quashing almost every entertaining and worldly satisfaction desired by mankind, Solomon powerfully concludes his observations: *"The end of the matter;*

---

[33] Ecclesiastes 3:11.

all has been heard. Fear God and keep his commandments, for this is the whole duty of man. [34]

In the book of Ecclesiastes King Solomon gives us a profound if subtle hint as to why we may not be satisfied, a clue you may easily miss when he writes in chapter 3: *"He [God] has put eternity into man's heart."* [35]

We have a deep yearning-desire that seemingly can't be satisfied in this world. What we truly desire is to be at home with our Father.

It reminds me of my ministry with high profile athletes. I find that many athletes dream of achieving athletic success. They give their whole life to that achievement, hoping the success will give them identity, happiness, and satisfaction. The few that actually achieve "the next level of success" do receive a certain amount of satisfaction, and yet the satisfaction is short-lived, and the athlete needs another level of success to get that feeling back. Many of the athletes I have worked with have climbed the ladder to the top and have been bewildered that the deep satisfaction promised at the next level had evaporated. Some athletes never get it: they seem to live in the past; others realize their ladder to achieve happiness has been set on the wrong wall.

As a youngster, I was chasing the sports dream. I thought, "If only I could achieve a certain level of success, then I could define myself as a successful person... then I would be happy." There was an emptiness in my heart that could only be satisfied by God. I tried to fill that gnawing emptiness with sport.

FOR CONTEMPLATION:

"Longing" has been a beautiful theme for writers, including Plato, Augustine, and C. S. Lewis. If we were merely an advanced set of atoms, would we have such longings deeply seated in our heart? Solomon wrote: *"He has put eternity into man's heart..."* [36] The search to satisfy those longings can be an excellent disciple-making starting point.

- How can you help your disciples to understand that the great yearning we have in the human heart is only satisfied with a deep friendship/lordship with God?

---

[34] Ecclesiastes 12:13.
[35] Ecclesiastes 3:11.
[36] Ecclesiastes 3:11.

- The more we realize that our seat of joy is in a healthy relationship with God, all the other beautiful longings that we chase will become reprioritized. What priorities do you need to reevaluate?

At the beginning of a disciple-making relationship, I often ask the person:
- "What are your dreams; what do you want; what are you deeply longing for?"

I get a variety of answers. But simply asking the question helps the disciple to connect with his longing. Plus, you can't give directions until you know where he is, and where he truly wants to go. I am amazed at how often people say to me: "Nobody has ever asked me that question before!"

Chapter 5
Rugged Love: God Sends His Love in Unique Forms—in My Case, It Was an Ex-Marine with a Whistle

"One thing I have observed in all my years of ministry is that the most effective and important aspects of evangelism usually take place on an individual, personal level. Most people do not come to Christ as an immediate response to a sermon they hear in a crowded setting. They come to Christ because of the influence of an individual."[37]

"A coach will influence more people in a year than an average person will in a lifetime."[38]

"You call me Teacher and Lord, and you are right, for so I am. If I then, your Lord and Teacher, have washed your feet, you also ought to wash one another's feet. For I have given you an example, that you also should do just as I have done to you."[39]

Jesus said, *"I have given you an example, that you also should do just as I have done to you."*[40] It is easy to get caught up in Jesus' methodology, and sometimes miss the message. Washing feet was a practical exercise in Jesus' culture. This was done by servants. Jesus models serving out of love with humility. It is the beginning of disciple-making.

What is a practical way you can serve others out of love today? What would happen if you asked your neighbor if you could wash his/her feet today? It probably would not go down too well. But there are a number of ways to humbly serve. Perhaps it is merely having someone over for coffee and listening to him. Maybe it is cleaning leaves from a neighbor's gutters, or fixing some kid's car or computer. Perhaps you might

---

[37] John MacArthur, The Vanishing Conscience.
[38] Fellowship of Christian Athletes, attributed to Billy Graham.
[39] John 13:13-15.
[40] John 13:15.

try icing a chubby kid's swollen ankle. You never know what an impression you might make.
If sport is your God, then your guru will be your coach. I would never have imagined as a boy what an influence a ball and an old man with a whistle would have on my life. My dad was a hard-bitten alcoholic, a world record skydiver,

> I would never have imagined as a boy what an influence a ball and an old man with a whistles would have on my life.

and a tough-as-nails ironworker from Chicago. I wanted to be just like my dad. Though my father made his living on the skyscrapers of Chicago, he was a country boy at heart. His favorite skydiving center was "out in the country;" a good 50 miles west of Chicago. So, Dad dragged us out of Chicago to the most unlikely environment for men and boys who love to swear, fight, and jump out of airplanes. He moved us to "The Holy City" (Wheaton, Illinois) so he could be closer to his favorite skydiving center.

Underneath my wannabe tough guy exterior was a painfully shy and insecure kid. Moving to a town that had at one time been in the *Guinness Book of World Records* for having the most churches per capita was a tricky thing for God to do. My dad warned me that "there were a lot of Holy Joes in this town." I didn't know what a Holy Joe was, but I didn't like the sound of it, so I kept my distance; and a lot of the Holy Joes kept their distance from me, too.

My mom had schizophrenia, so I did not know her very well. It was tough on a fat kid's self-esteem when your mom walked through the streets of a middle-class neighborhood, smoking and talking to herself. My mom's mental illness was somewhat overlooked in Chicago, but out in the Holy Land, it could be embarrassing. Our new life in the suburbs included fights, police issues, getting kicked out of Boy Scouts, and suspension from school! It took only one year for my life to turn sour.

In addition, my parents' marriage slowly, and at times violently, eroded, and finally ended in divorce. My sister and I lived with Mom, who was in and out of the mental health hospital—and was the cause of being the butt of many jokes.

Whenever I would hear those jokes, I would pretend to laugh, but my gut would retch. Eventually, my sister and I started bouncing around with Dad, grandparents, and friends.

Later in college, I learned that my family would be considered "dysfunctional." Of course, when you grow up in the craziness, you don't call it dysfunction: you think it is normal. Normal for me: I enjoyed fighting, skipping school, and hanging around with skydivers. I still do (hanging around with skydivers, that is), but the loss of parents, God's perfect plans for discipleship—now that hurt. The 17th-century French mathematician and philosopher Blaise Pascal wrote in his journal Pensées (Thoughts): *"There is a God-shaped vacuum in the heart of every man which cannot be filled by any created thing, but only by God, the Creator, made known through Jesus."*[41] I had a "vacuum" in my heart the size of Lake Michigan.

Fast forward: over the past three decades, I have discipled many high-profile and professional athletes. I see the same thing all the time. The guys are all trying to fill the God-shaped vacuum in their lives with things TV commercials promise will bring them happiness and fulfillment. We dream of those things; we run for those things; and sometimes we even achieve those things. Those things—whether it is a new car, new shoes, a new team, or new women—can make us deliriously happy for about a week. In the long run, however, they do not satisfy. The true reality is found in the words of a modern philosopher (well he ain't that modern anymore) Mick Jagger when he sings: "I Can't Get No Satisfaction."[42] Even if many of those things we chase are wonderful and make our lives better, they ultimately don't fill the vacuum in our heart, which only Jesus was made for.

I had a hole in my heart, which I tried to fill. I was shy, inarticulate, insecure, and angry. One thing I seemed to have going for me was an aptitude for knocking people over, yet being able to knock people over has little long-term intrinsic value. For example, it never helped my golf game or my chess game; and it certainly never helped keep me on the right pitch when

---

[41] Blaise Pascal, Pensées.
[42] The Rolling Stones, "Satisfaction," 1965.

singing in church. What knocking people over did give me was a little attention from football coaches. For an unsocial kid with emptiness in his heart, any attention, positive or negative, was a lifeline.

The only rule I remember having in my life before meeting my high school coach was "don't get caught," and if you got into difficulty: lie. I learned that I was to deny everything if ever in trouble, and to be sneaky. Again, do what you want, but don't get caught! It was fair to say that there was not much discipline in my life.

Though I liked skydiving, my passion had become football. I had no choice in one thing: if I was to try to fulfill the emptiness that I thought being a football player would satisfy, I had to be involved with the gatekeeper to that world. That gatekeeper was my high school football coach, Coach Rexilius, who was known as Coach Rex. He was a no-nonsense ex-Marine and seemed ancient and scary. He also had a lot of rules.

Most of Coach Rex's rules were running counter to everything I had learned so far in life. I remember reading an article written about Coach Rexilius in a Chicago newspaper that was headlined: "The King of Discipline." I never thought I would enjoy discipline but was surprised to find that I did. When you were part of Coach Rex's team, you were immersed in a program full of rules. I cycled through the emotions of hating his rules; to using his rules (to get what I wanted); to loving his rules; and then back to hating his rules. "Get your hair cut." "Be on time." "Never, ever lie." "Treat people with respect." "Give 110 percent." That one really confused me in math class.

In Rex's football program, I felt simultaneously safe and frightened with him. Rex was never prideful, but there was an unrelenting passion for winning and excellence. It seemed like my life was lived in two parallel universes. I would go to the skydiving drop-zone, meet my dad, and hang out in a "whatever-felt-good-doit" lifestyle. Then I would be back into Coach Rex's world, which was full of discipline and boundaries.

My first impression was that Coach Rex was one of an ogre. I had never seen an ogre, but if I did, I was sure it would look like Rex. I assumed that anyone with that many rules would not like me, or for that matter, would not like anyone. I understood that if I was to achieve anything in football, I had to tolerate the rules and the coach.

> I assumed that anyone with that many rules would not like me, or for that matter, would not like anyone.

Rex had great football teams. He did not merely build a "program": he created an expectation of excellence in the lives of his athletes, which manifested into success. He certainly brought discipline and sound technique, as well as advanced training into his system. However, his genius was the convergence of toughness and discipline with one seemingly counterintuitive ingredient that made toughness and discipline come alive: *rugged* love! He loved us! Coach Rex's coaching staff bought into his philosophy, too. Toughness and *rugged* love permeated his teams. Many players on his teams are still my close friends.

He wasn't perfect, however, and sometimes his hard-nosed strictness was to a fault. Nevertheless, his strange, *rugged* love was foundational to his life and sports programs. I more fully understand Rex's *rugged* love, but if high expectations and running "gassers" until I wanted to puke was love, it seemed like a strange way to show it. I did not understand then where Rex's *rugged* love came from, but over time I got used to it, and started to become attracted to it; like coming out of a dark room into a bright light, it takes a few seconds to adjust your eyes.

David Maraniss' great book, *When Pride Still Mattered*, is a useful examination of the great Green Bay head football coach Vince Lombardi's *rugged* love. The author observes Lombardi's motives, which reflect many coaches who have a spiritual foundation and a similar approach. He quotes Lombardi: *"It was what God wanted, the sincerest expression of holiness. We have God-given talents, and are expected to use them to our fullest whenever we play."*[43] The profound but often ignored admonition that everything we do should glorify God, signals that each individual performance is tied to a higher calling; and we glorify God the most when we "put out" the most in whatever occupation or profession we have chosen.

---

[43] David Maraniss, *When Pride Still Mattered*, 1999.

Like Lombardi, Coach Rex drove us hard, and many teammates quit. However, many of those who stuck it out went on to successful football careers in college, the NFL, and successful careers in numerous other occupations. Rex not only prepared us for football, but more importantly, for life. He did this in many ways that we would not understand until much later. In retrospect, we learned not to be intimidated by adversity, and to courageously pursue the challenges of life. He gave me a sense that we were "made for huge, *rugged* adventures."

When playing for Coach Rex, I had a sense that there was something bigger and more important behind his brutal practices and occasional tongue-lashings. I did not recognize it at the time, but it was Rex's commitment to God and his love for his athletes that drove him to excellence.

What really attracted me to him was the interest he took in me as a person. Once, as a freshman, I sprained my ankle, and was sitting in the cramped, makeshift training room, trying to ice my leg. Rex came in, grabbed the ice, and worked it over the knot that had ballooned on the back of my Achilles tendon. He sat there, talking to me, and asking about my family. I was shivering, but it was more from being around the great man/ogre than the ice.

On another occasion, Rex called me into his office and said, "Here is a pair of shoes I got out of the lost and found box. Do you want them? I will throw them away if you don't."

"Yeah, I want them!" I said, trying to hide my excitement. They were beautiful and fit perfectly. I had been trying to glue my old shoes back together, but to my embarrassment, the front part of the sole kept coming off, flapping as I walked down the halls of my high school. This was not the best way to impress girls. He gave me the shoes in his cramped little coach's office (I like the smell of a coach's office—they usually have the smell of being a kid and the smell of being a man all mixed together). After this, he left to teach a PE class— Rex would let me hang out in his office where I would pretend to do homework. As I daydreamed, staring at the mysterious recruiting posters of college football programs, in my 45minute "study session," I noticed a price tag and a new shoe box in his garbage can. Rex had bought me a pair of shoes, and pretended they were from the lost and found. I took the shoe box out and put it in my locker to hold my stuff. I can't tell you how proud I was of those new shoes, and what that shoe box represented to me. That shoe box represented love.

POSTSCRIPT:

When you were involved with Rex, you were in an environment of leadership development. Whether you wanted it or not, you were immersed in an incubator of *rugged* love. Now an incubator is a device that is used to create an atmosphere that is helpful to protect, maintain, and encourage growth. Any atmosphere that promotes healthy human growth needs love. In retrospect, I see Rex's football program closer to Jesus' model of discipleship with His disciples than many of our church's anemic attempts to make disciples.

Wherever He went, Jesus created an environment that protected truth and encouraged real authentic love. When I observe Jesus' training of the Twelve, He seemed to generate an atmosphere, a sort of mobile incubator, of *rugged* love, which challenged men and women wherever He went. Jesus drove His disciples hard and challenged them often. His training had little resemblance to our modern-day "discipleship classes." If you were in His presence, you were in an incubator of total human growth. Jesus dared His disciples to mature—mentally, spiritually, physically, and socially. His environment was not based on mere lecture, though He was the Master Teacher. He modeled that *rugged* love in their lives.

We are also called to be "mobile incubators," taking the influence of Jesus' *rugged* love and intentional discipleship wherever we go, not just to a "discipleship class" once a week. When I look at modern-day discipleship, sitting in an air-conditioned church classroom, eating donuts, and memorizing the Greek word for church, it really does not resemble Jesus' training program. Coach Rex's discipleship may look unconventional to many modern disciple-making processes we see today, but it arguably contained several authentic ingredients of Jesus' young team of the Twelve.

God places a high value on human beings. If He didn't, then why did He allow His Son to be sacrificed for them? Jesus said in the parable of the talents: *"Everyone to whom much was given, of him much will be required, and from him to whom they entrusted much, they will demand the more.*[44] What can be more critical than when you have been entrusted with lives? God puts people in our world for a purpose. Coach Rex understood that he was entrusted with young lives, and with his limited skills and resources, Coach Rex tried to make the best of what God had given him.

For good or bad, I think a coach has the potential to be the second most influential person in a young man's life, next to his father. Yet sadly, a coach can be the most influential person in his life if the dad abdicates his God-ordained entrusted role of a father.

It has been well-documented that the influence a male role model can have on a youth, either positive or negative, is compelling. This is exceptionally true in the highly relational nature of sport. It is a misconception that sport automatically builds character, but it indeed does reveal character. What coaches do and don't do, send critically positive and negative life lessons to young people. A coach's priorities may never be articulated, but his/her actions, subtly and directly, reveal both character and priorities.

> A coach's priorities may never be articulated, but his/her actions, subtly and directly, reveal both character and priorities.

I am shocked at how many Christians, especially men in influential roles (it doesn't have to be as a coach), who don't leverage their influence for Kingdom impact. Who better to disciple youth in the world of sport than a coach? Who better to disciple a musician than another musician? Who better to disciple a businessman than the owner of a business?

Some people I meet understand their role and take the responsibilities given to them very seriously. Sadly, they seem to be the minority. I am amazed to see youth coaches who serve their church faithfully in the role as an elder or deacon, but never bring their faith strategically into the God-entrusted responsibility as a coach. Nor do many churches wholeheartedly encourage us to serve outside the church walls. Let me also say that this is not

---

[44] Luke 12:48.

just a problem in the American church. This is endemic cancer to the church all over the world.

I will go so far as to say that I think many Christian men are cowards and are ashamed to express their faith in their sphere of influence. In Luke, Jesus says, *"For whosoever is ashamed of me and of my words, of him will the Son of Man be ashamed when he comes in his glory and in the glory of the Father and of the holy angels."*[45]

It has been recognized over and over that most people come to Christ and grow in Him through a relationship, not a great sermon. When we observe Jesus with the disciples, a key ingredient left out of most modern discipleship programs is authentic relationships underscored by *rugged* love. We understand the proclamation ingredient of the gospel, but many of our church discipleship programs seem almost entirely devoid of reliable relationships, which lead to authentic and *rugged* love. We know more about the lives of movie stars than we do the lives of the people around us. Jesus ate, slept, sailed, and walked with His disciples. It was those actions that created relationship and love.

Our challenge as we make disciples will be to create an atmosphere of love and relationship in a very busy, yet isolated world. I am a speaker, trainer, and writer, but over time, I have come to realize that the most significant influence I can have is finding people to rub shoulders with. What most people want is to be loved.

In that small training room, I was surprised that a busy head football coach would make time to get to know me and ice my ankle. It was a practical response to Jesus' words: *"For I have given you an example, that you also should do just as I have done to you."*[46] I don't remember much of my high school days, but I do remember that moment like it was yesterday. I started to build a relationship with that old coach which would impact me for eternity. I began to feel Jesus' love strangely manifested through a former Marine and a cup of ice.

FOR CONTEMPLATION:

---

45 Luke 9:26.
46 John 13:15.

40

I used to think that discipleship was best done in a classroom face-to-face, but now I realize it is best done in a relationship, shoulder-to-shoulder.

- How can you best respond to when Jesus says, *"I have set you an example that you should do as I have done for you."*[47]
- Whom has God put in your life for you to encourage "shoulder-to-shoulder"? It may be a young athlete, or perhaps someone across the hall in your dormitory, barracks, or company.
- It is no coincidence that a person has been put in your sphere of influence. How can you show authentic, intentional Christian love to that person today?

---

[47] John 13:15.

Chapter 6
Rugged Truth: It Will Not Return to Me Empty

"How beautiful upon the mountains are the feet of him who brings good news, who publishes peace, who brings good news of happiness, who publishes salvation, who says to Zion, Your God reigns!"[48]

"For as the rain and the snow come down from heaven and do not return there but water the earth, making it bring forth and sprout, giving seed to the sower and bread to the eater, so shall my word be that goes out from my mouth; it shall not return to me empty, but it shall accomplish that which I purpose, and shall succeed in the thing for which I sent it."[49]

The Power of Scripture

Because of the small talent I had for knocking people over, I fell in love with the game of football. The sport was more than a passion for me—it became my god. Fortunately, if football was my god, my high school football coach was my guru. He was a former Marine, and when Coach Rex told me to jump, I said: "How high?" When he said: "Run," I said: "How far?" When he said: "I want you to go to an FCA (Fellowship of Christian Athletes) camp this summer," I asked: "What is FCA, Future Coaches of America?" Coach Rex said: "Yeah, kinda, but mainly it will be good for you!"

So, I went. Whether I knew it or not, I had just been adopted by a spiritual father, one who wore a Marine-style flat-top haircut. My life was about to change. I had to get a haircut too!

I don't really know if Coach Rex had a systematic theological plan for making disciples, but he was driven by his *rugged* love of Christ, and that drive pushed him towards obedience to His God.

---

[48] Isaiah 52:7.
[49] Isaiah 55:10, 11.

Being an ex-Marine, he knew how to take orders. So when Jesus said: "Go... and make disciples," he obeyed.[50]

Coach Rex combined humility with an unrelenting hunger for excellence. These were byproducts of his love for Jesus Christ— byproducts that made him one of the most respected (and winning) coaches in his state.

For his entire football-coaching career, he would sacrifice part of his short summer to take his athletes and coaching staff to a Fellowship of Christian Athletes camp somewhere in America. We would pile on buses and make the journey to some college campus. Our high school athletes would mix at camp with people who were different from us—different accents, different skin, and different ideas. For me, these trips were both exciting and horrible.

C. S. Lewis described his conversion to Christianity while a lecturer at Oxford University. His thoughts represented many of our own feelings as we struggled to put our trust and life in God's hands.

"You must picture me alone in that room in Magdalen, night after night, feeling, whenever my mind lifted even for a second from my work, the steady, unrelenting approach of Him whom I so earnestly desired not to meet. That which I greatly feared had at last come upon me. In the Trinity Term of 1929, I gave in, and admitted that God was God, and knelt and prayed: perhaps, that night, the most dejected and reluctant convert in all England."[51]

To be honest, I had no clue what I was getting into at that first FCA camp in central Michigan. I loved the swimming pool and showing off with crazy stunts on the high dive. I was very much looking forward to hearing and meeting the professional athletes that were reported to be coming to the camp. What I assumed would be the "religious" segment did not interest me. I figured the pro-athletes would talk about sport, and some preacher would bore me with a "God slot" in the camp schedule which I was determined to ignore. I made up my mind that when those "Holy Joes" got up to speak, I was not going to listen.

---

[50] Matthew 28:19ff.

[51] C. S. Lewis, *Surprised by Joy.*

43

Many of us feared, loved, and respected Coach Rex. We reluctantly acquiesced to his invitation to attend a Christian sports camp, but religion was not for me. Like C. S. Lewis, I also "earnestly desired not to meet [God]." I asked myself: "What would my dad think if I got religious? What would my skydiving friends think?" My youthful pride could think of nothing more repulsive than admitting I needed help. There was maybe one thing worse than realizing I needed help, and it was giving my life over to God's rules. I'd heard that the Bible frowned on sex before marriage. I was a virgin, but I was determined that I was not going to last!

The first speaker on the first night of camp was an NFL (National Football League) quarterback, the next a massive offensive lineman. I was immediately disarmed by their regular-guy attitude. Even more confusing was that they talked about Jesus, and they talked about Him as if they knew Him! I figured that they would, at best, talk about what Jesus did, or what He said. I thought they would approach Jesus as a person to admire from history.

I can tell you where Abraham Lincoln was on November 19, 1863 (Gettysburg, Pennsylvania), and what he said. "Four score and seven years ago our fathers brought forth on this continent, a new nation, conceived in Liberty..." I can tell you how that affected my life as an American, but I don't know Abraham Lincoln personally. So, it struck me as odd, but also intriguing, that these athletes whom I immediately respected, spoke of a personal friendship with a man who also claimed to be the "Son of God," and lived 2000 years ago. Some of these professional athletes were talking as if they knew Jesus personally, and some of them seemed to know Him really well.

For me, the most memorable speaker at that first FCA camp was the legendary Paul Anderson, a 1956 Olympic Gold Medalist and world champion powerlifter. Anderson did several amazing "feats of strength," which shattered my impression that Christians were "wimps." (Do we use that word anymore?) Every time I remember Anderson's bold signature line, I smile. *"I'm the strongest man in the world. If I can't live one day without Jesus Christ, how do you think you can?"* As I sat on a folded chair in that crowded and hot gymnasium not far from where

Anderson was speaking, it felt like he was pointing and speaking right at me! *"How do you think you can?"* All could I say to myself was: "Good point."

The *rugged* speakers at the camp, for the most part, had good stories that pulled the rug out from under all those "Holy Joe" prejudices that I had tried to cling to. I may not have believed in God, but I could not deny that the speakers and many of the young athletes at that camp were influenced by and passionate about their God. It was an uncomfortable and compelling experience.

Personal stories are not enough, however, that is to become an authentic follower of Jesus Christ. The Apostle Paul, inspired by God, wrote: "So faith comes from hearing, and hearing through the word of Christ."[52] It is God's revealed Word, working through the Holy Spirit, that makes a potent cocktail: especially when combined with personal stories of transformation.

> It is God's revealed Word, working through the Holy Spirit, that makes a potent cocktail: especially when combined with personal stories of transformation.

Fortunately, my coach knew athletes' stories (also known as "testimonies," another churchy word I did not understand) were important, but they were not enough. Personal faith in a living God, who had become a man, was still a real disconnect to me; but there had been something nagging at my heart ever since I'd seen my friend Twink die in that cornfield several years earlier.

I had no idea Coach Rex was "religious." He did not fit the bill for what my dad called a "Holy Joe." After all, he wore goofy, old-fashioned sweat suits, and he yelled at us a lot. I thought religious people wore fancy clothes, and never raised their voices! I just figured he took us to camp in the summer to keep his athletes in shape and out of trouble.

My stereotype of a Christian was slowly changing, but I still assumed Christianity was merely conforming to a dress code; some choice language alterations; perhaps giving up "sleeping in" on Sundays to go church; and studying about Jesus from a history book. It seemed to me being a Christian just meant

---

[52] Romans 10:17.

buying some nice clothes, taking time out of your weekend to sing irrelevant songs, and listening to some priest or preacher tell you how to react to bad people.

I thought a sports camp was going to be fun, but I was mostly miserable. Something deep inside me was fighting a battle. A steady, unrelenting force was at work in my heart. The Holy Spirit's collision with what Jesus called "salt and light" to my young dark soul was horrible. I did not recognize it, but there was a war waging in my soul with larger-than-life consequences.

Fortunately for me, Coach Rex understood genuine transformation was much more than not cussing and going to church. During free time at camp, Rex sat me down, and quietly explained to me the gospel message. Rex told why Jesus died on the "cross," and the consequences of sin. I am amazed at how we Christians are afraid to mention sin. If humans were not sinners, why would we need a Savior? Then he opened up his Bible to a strange book titled Romans. I thought to myself: "What did I have in common with Romans? I thought Jesus was Jewish, anyhow!" He turned to a passage and read it slowly, in an easy-to-understand version of Scripture: *"For the wages of sin is death, but the free gift of God is eternal life in Christ Jesus our Lord."*[53] He exerted no pressure on me at all. He just let the Scripture speak, and the Holy Spirit go to work.

Coach Rex did not have to expound on sin to me, as I was pretty good at that, but it was awful to hear that my sin was an incurable disease and would put me in hell. The only remedy is to admit I had the disease, and trust that "God is God, and would put all things right!" God dealt with sin by personally paying the ultimate price, by sacrificing His own amazing Son. Coach Rex went on to explain in simple terms that God did not want me to be "the king of the world." Instead, God wanted to be the Head Coach in my life.

I wish I could tell you that at that moment, I had a Damascus road experience (immediate scales falling from my eyes). I did not, and inwardly I fought like hell (literally) to stay away from Jesus. When Rex asked me if I had "given my life to Christ," I answered him the way I was trained to: I lied! I told him: "Yeah, I am a Christian." I'd say anything to get God and Rex off

---

[53] Romans 6:23.

my back, and hopefully stop this war that was raging in my gut! Coach Rex must have had a bunch of old grannies praying for us, because I could not shake the appeal to "know" Jesus; "the steady, unrelenting approach of Him." I thought my coach had zeroed in on me because I was apparently a pretty bad sinner. Later, I learned he had systematically presented the gospel in some way to almost every kid that he took to camp.

Throughout the week, athletes and coaches were invited to walk to the front of the gym and follow Jesus. I learned this was called an "altar call." What kind of "altar" is in a gym?

God's overwhelming love was the force that troubled me: a love that was first manifested through my old coach and his passion for God. There comes the point in many lives when the awareness of grace (unmerited love) starts to break down your pride. Everything I heard my entire young life underscored the concept of being self-reliant. I tried to convince myself by saying: "Just start being a better person: you don't need help; if there is a God, He will be cool with that." Yet when I considered what value I could bring to God's table, I realized I had nothing good to deliver Him. Slowly, I became aware of the bitter fact that I needed a Savior.

It was hard to imagine myself living a life with God. It seemed so constricting, and yet I kept wrestling with those verses from Romans 6: *"For the wages of sin is death..."* I kept thinking about Paul Anderson's quote: *"If I can't live one day without Jesus, how do you think you can?"*

When you wrestle with God, you first have to lose to win. I really didn't have much to surrender as a 15-year-old, but what I had, I gave to God. Romans 6:23, *"the free gift of God,"* was piercing my heart. I knew I did not deserve such a gift, and only my pride was standing in the way of taking it. On the second-to-last day of camp, I ran back to my dorm room, and finally, like C. S. Lewis, *"admitted that God was God, and knelt and prayed. That night I was, perhaps, the most dejected and reluctant convert"* in the entire world of sport. Later, I would understand that there were external and internal forces battling for my soul. I also learned that the angels were about to dance!

My paradigm was shifting from self-determination ("do whatever you want, just don't get caught"), to living a life of faith and obedience with the Creator of the universe. I was learning that there was an omnipotent power that likes to be addressed as Abba (Dear Father). Make no mistake, it was a slow transformation. When I invited Christ into my life, I wondered if I would see lightning or hear some thunder; and yet neither occurred. I was determined that if my reluctant heart was going to submit to God, I was not going to make a fuss about joining God's team. I said a quiet prayer in my dorm room and tried to forget the whole thing.

A couple of weeks later, I told Coach Rex what had happened. I hadn't realized it at the time, but I was starting to "participate in the divine nature." I hoped that Rex wouldn't make a big deal out of my "conversion." He didn't. That autumn, Rex just yelled at me a bit more, and pushed me to be more of a leader. I saw that as a good sign. He showed his love for me by expecting more out of me. He also gave me a big, fat study Bible.

Over the years, I have observed that some people gravitate towards an incomplete process of disciple-making. Some people really connect with "building relationships," but are undisciplined or intimidated to speak *rugged* truth of God's Word into the lives they wish to disciple. Some people really connect with the power of "the Word," but are either afraid of or can't be bothered to build relationships. Both are essential. Jesus modeled and valued developing relationships and speaking truth.

I have to admit, theoretically speaking, if I were forced only to use one tool for making disciples (which I am not), it would be teaching my disciples to devour the Bible. I am amazed at how some people will build incredible relationships with the people they want to disciple, and yet rarely study God's authoritative, living Word! God's revealed truth is the authority, and central to a human's transformation! I am also saddened that many Bible teachers have little or no authentic relationships with those they call their disciples. That is not Jesus' way.

The place and role of Scripture is core to discipleship. If we do not train our disciples to understand the need to devour the Scriptures, we are not doing discipleship. We are merely forming a social club. If the Word of God is not central to our disciples' daily nourishment, we are generating lackluster, feeble Christians who may do more harm than good.

Over his career, Coach Rex's influence on athletes and coaches was unprecedented. He had what many would describe as an "aura" around him. Wherever he went, you sensed he was bringing an atmosphere, a sort of "mobile incubator," of tough love and truth. Some of the elements in his "mobile incubator" included passion, an expectation for excellence, and a desire

> *If we do not train our disciples to understand the need to devour the Scriptures, we are not doing discipleship. We are merely forming a social club.*

for getting the best out of his players and teams. What he really brought, which was pure dynamite, was the truth: God's Word. Rex always bought a stack of Bibles, and gave them away, every chance he got.

Some people loved Coach Rex. Some people really didn't like him at all, but rarely have I met people that did not respect him. I have spent much of my professional life as a player, coach, and pastor/chaplain, and Rex's aura ("mobile incubator") and his sphere of influence remains. His was the most dynamic and the most effective I have ever observed.

Nonetheless, Coach Rex had a dilemma. He knew he could not disciple every kid on his team. He understood that those players needed to be rooted in a community of Christ-followers. An answer to part of his problem was about to arrive with a southern accent and a body like a bulldog.

POSTSCRIPT:

The Scriptures at the beginning of the chapter were written by a man called Isaiah. Isaiah was a prophet; he had a unique contact with our God and was guided to speak (scribe) on His behalf. He was a spokesperson for the Creator of the universe, and he did it for over six decades. Isaiah's task was to convey a message from God of eternal truth, guidance, and warning. This makes up a part of what we call the Word of God, or the Bible. Isaiah's description and predictions of Jesus (approximately 700 years before His birth) are extraordinary, inspiring, and encouraging. God tells us that His Word is powerful and supernatural. God tells us that His Word will *"accomplish that which I purpose, and shall succeed in the thing for which I sent it."*[54]

Many of the Biblical prophets had a *rugged* time. Not everybody wants to hear the truth. As disciple-makers, our job is to bring God's Word to our potential disciples. Sharing God's Word is an awe-inspiring duty. But not everybody is going to love the messenger. I certainly did not want to hear the truth.

FOR CONTEMPLATION:

I used to think we needed famous people to tell us about Jesus. Now I realize we need average people speaking God's Word to make Jesus famous.

- Nobody is asking you to be a Bible professor, but are you actively learning God's Word?
- Are you intentionally providing those you are discipling with a working knowledge of Scripture?
- Sometimes all we need are small steps forward. I like to encourage those I disciple to find a Scripture they can memorize, which will be a theme for a season of their life. That small step will open up more Scripture and reveal more truth that they can live by.
- What Bible verse could you use memorize with those you are discipling today?

I don't recommend this, but one of my guys tattooed the Scripture on his arm! Let's tattoo Scriptures to our hearts!

---

[54] Isaiah 55:11.

Chapter 7
Rugged Harvest: Let's Grow

"Then he said to his disciples, 'The harvest is plentiful, but the laborers are few; therefore pray earnestly to the Lord of the harvest to send out laborers into his harvest.'"[55]

Weight Coach and Church Coach

It may be common knowledge that weight and cardio training are essential to becoming a better athlete, yet for me as a high school youth in the late seventies, fitness was a total mystery to me. Reps, sets, resistance-training, progression, avoiding a plateau, muscle recovery, and nutrition all sounded like cryptic words of a secret society. It could be an intimidating experience walking into our high school's weight room. I actually felt as if I was entering a strange temple: some type of holy place. It was an odd sanctuary which I was a bit intimidated to enter.

Our weight room was a small, converted classroom. It had a musty smell of old sweat and steel. Many of the weights looked like they were smuggled out of Cold War Russia. I was in awe at the strength and power of many of the upperclassmen. Of course, I wanted to be that powerful, but hadn't a clue how to progress. In all the weight rooms I have worked out in, there are always unwritten rules, procedures, and etiquette. I would learn these sacred protocols the hard way, usually by getting yelled at: "Connor, get the blankety-blank out of the way."

I understood getting bigger, faster, and stronger was imperative for me if I was to become a better athlete. My dilemma was that I had not yet been taught the disciplines or the science of strength and speed training. My dream of transforming myself into an explosive defender was not working. I would do a few curls and look and see if my chubby arms had immediately turned into ripped, bulging sinew. They hadn't. I would lift weights for hours, jump out of bed the next morning, and gaze in the mirror, hoping I looked like a bodybuilder. Nope, nothing! What I needed was a weight coach!

---

[55] Matthew 9:37, 38.

51

The other daunting mystery in my life as a youth was my embryonic faith and the strange institution called "church." Though I wanted to grow as an athlete, I had no clue that I could also grow as a Christian: nor did I have any strong desire to do so. Walking into the weight room as an underclassman was intimidating enough, walking into a church was terrifying. Words like altar call, quiet time, evangelical, testimony, and communion, again seemed like cryptic words of a secret society. Trying to navigate the new Bible Coach Rex had given me was embarrassing. When I heard the pastor say, "Turn to Matthew," I looked in the church for a guy called Matthew. I felt completely lost. It seemed hopeless as I watched people easily turn to the Gospel called Matthew. How did they know this?

> *Walking into the weight room as an underclassman was intimidating enough, walking into a church was terrifying.*

Like the weight room, the church also had a mysterious set of procedures and etiquette. When I did something wrong in the weight room, I was immediately corrected. In the church, if I stood at the wrong time or said something inappropriate, I was only given a watery smile, which I had to interpret for myself. I needed a church coach!

I wanted to be a great athlete and emulate many of the upperclassmen in my high school. Sadly, the few Christians I met in my rare excursions to church did not inspire me to want to be like them. I do not want to beat up the church in America, or anywhere in the world, for that matter. All I am saying is that as a young believer, I had very few relationships with authentic Christians. What I thought was an authentic Christian, I had no desire to imitate. It is a good reminder for me today as I attempt to make disciples. Am I an example of someone who really enjoys God's love? Do I have a Christ-centered faith that is infectious and worthy to follow and emulate?

One day while I was struggling in our weight room to get a few pounds over my head, a new guy called Jack appeared. Jack was an anomaly. He was built like a pit bull, but as friendly as a Labrador. He had swagger, but no attitude. He walked around the place with ease, as if he was born in an iron pit, and the man was strong!

My friends and I just assumed Jack was some sort of factory worker who must have just got off the night shift, and needed a place to work out. We figured Coach Rex, our patriarchal football coach, grudgingly allowed him to use the facilities during the day. What was even more appealing about Jack was that he had a mysterious southern accent. He used strange sounding words like "bro" and "get-er-done." We learned he was a Georgia Bulldog.

The first real encounter I had with Jack was while I was attempting to do some leg squats. I put on more weight on the bar than was good for me. My form was atrocious, and I must have looked pitiful. My attempt to look like a tough guy failed. So, if you can't work out like a tough guy, the next best thing (I thought) was pretend to act like a tough guy. I was swearing under my breath (hoping Coach Rex did not hear me), looking angry, and acting like I was just having a bad day—and I expected to make the lift. As I took a break, Jack approached me and, with a toothy grin, said, "Hey, big man, my name is Jack. Do ya wanna work out with me, bro? I could use a spot."

Now Jack, was all of 5' 9", but back then he was taller than me, and a whole lot stronger! I immediately turned around and looked behind me, figuring he was asking one of the seniors, certainly not me. Nope, no one behind me: he must be talking to me. I asked myself, "Where was this guy from? Why did he want to bother with me?" I hesitantly said: "Uhhh, okay." If you ever meet Jack, I recommend that you do not work out with him unless you want to feel sore—I mean, really, really sore—the next day. We started to train together, and I began to get a bit stronger. More importantly however, and to my surprise, he wanted to be my friend.

It was quite a shock when I found out later that Jack was actually not a night shift factory worker at all, but an assistant pastor at a small, humble church in our community. He had wrestled at University of Georgia, and had worked with a Christian sports movement called Athletes in Action. Nonetheless, his heart was in the church and making disciples. He had recently become a youth pastor in our town.

Jack loved athletes, and soon after moving into the community, he heard that there was an outspoken Christian coach called Rex, a man who was teaching and coaching in one of the local high schools. Jack had heard about the legendary, if a bit crusty, football coach who had been taking athletes to a Christian sports camp. He was determined to meet him and offer his help.

For years every summer, Rex had been taking his athletes to a Christian sports camp somewhere in the United States. Coach Rex invited athletes to his house (across the street from our high school) for a weekly Fellowship of Christian Athletes meeting, usually every Thursday evening.

Rex was also sorely aware of both the power and weakness of a para-church ministry. Rex's FCA meetings were a great way to expose youth to Christ, as well as encouraging young Christians who were also athletes, but Coach Rex was very committed to the local church, and understood that a student's athletic career was short, and thus para-ministries like FCA influence would be short as well. He also realized that a local faith community, a local congregation, was vital if his student-athlete's faith was ever going to take root and grow spiritually. Years later, Rex would lament to me, "Where are all those kids now?"

So, Jack made his way to my high school as a young pastor and introduced himself to Coach Rex. He asked him:

"Is there anyone here who needs discipling?"

Rex quickly wisecracked, "The entire school needs discipling, but I recommend you start with the kids I just took to camp."

"Where are they?" Jack asked.

Rex replied, "They are in the weight room."

As I read the Bible, I can't find a verse which says that nonChristians should go to church, but I have recognized a most neglected and recurring theme: Believers should go to the lost. *"The harvest is plentiful..."*[56]

Jack had responded to Christ's command to "go" and make disciples. Jack could have been a world-class weightlifter, but he sacrificed that dream to become a world-class disciple-maker of young people. Instead of focusing on merely building his body, Jack used his passion (and gift) of weight training to

---

[56] Matthew 9:37.

build relationships with high school athletes, and help them to engage in a healthy, *rugged* life with Christ. The sweat Jack put out in the weight room was nothing like the *rugged* work it took for him to get a few of us rooted in our Christian faith. It was long, hard, intentional, sacrificial work. It took tender care, a few kicks in the butt, a load of time, several disappointments, and lots and lots of food!

Jack found a few tiny spiritual saplings in the weight room, and he started to cultivate them. I find it interesting that it was common for a first-century Jew to seek out a rabbi to be his teacher. In contrast, Jesus, after much prayer would intentionally recruit His disciples and call them individually.[57] It is a good reminder for us disciple-makers to ask God to send us to those He wants us to disciple. There are times that I have invested in the wrong person, motivated by the flesh instead of the Spirit, but we should keep pursuing those disciples God has prayerfully put into our hearts. It is a long hard road, but the payoff is eternally rewarding.

Jack invited us wannabe football players over to his house several times before he ever asked us to his church. We would crowd into his little home. His lovely young wife, Robin, would cook hot dogs and some excellent southern side dishes. She had a grace and hospitality that made us all feel like we were her long-lost friends. We would eat, hang around, and when their refrigerator was empty, take off.

I remember Jack eventually did ask us to "come and check out my Sunday school class. Y'all gonna love it!" We did not seriously think we would "love" going to school on a Sunday (we took the day of rest seriously!). I believe the only reason we started going to Jack's church was that we did not want to see him get fired. We loved him and his wife, Robin. We needed a weight coach and a free meal.

After putting it off for as long as we could, we finally did show up at Jack's Sunday school class. Our gang would pile out of my friend's old junk heap and wander over to where Jack was holding his class on the front porch of his church.

We started hearing Jack, on a semi-formal platform, speak about Jesus. He was an enthusiastic preacher, even if it was on the front porch of his church, but this was not the first time

---

57 Luke 6:12.

55

Jack ever talked to us about Jesus. He spoke informally about Him all the time, but his language and approach were usually conversational and in a casual, warmhearted manner. He would say, "Hey, bro, you are getting stronger: I see it every day. Is your life with Jesus getting stronger?" We would, of course, say yes, but we were not quite sure what that meant.

Over the spring and summer, we would sporadically go to his Sunday school. It was surprisingly good. We got to know the churchy kids, and they learned to tolerate our coming late, wearing shorts and T-shirts, and zooming off right after the lesson. We never went into the church itself, since Jack held his class on the front porch. We were certainly not consistent in our attendance, and that's something I have to remind myself of when I get frustrated with some of my own athletes who are not so regular for our Bible studies and chapels.

Jack was a great teacher, and over time he would root us in the foundational disciplines of spiritual maturity. He taught us how to have a quiet time, which he aptly called "power time." He helped us memorize Scripture, he encouraged us to stay close and encourage our spiritual teammates (fellowship), and he pounded into us the need to share our faith, which I was terrified to do. It took us until late autumn when it was too cold to meet outside before we finally stepped inside the church building.

What is remarkable, as I look back on my time with Jack, is how little I remember of him teaching us formally. We spent so much time with him that it was more the essence of the man, his love for Jesus, which slowly rubbed off on us. For instance, he would throw a spiritual pearl of wisdom our way while taking us to a movie. Jack would give us some Biblical encouragement while helping with our form on the bench press. He would teach us trust by allowing us to watch his young family (he was no fool: we were free babysitters!).

I remember how Jack treated poor and disenfranchised people with kindness and respect, and I remember how Jack treated his young wife, and how he treated his parents. Jack's life was his classroom. We would be with Jack when he talked to presidents of banks, or we would stand behind Jack when he spoke to Chicago gang leaders. He would speak of Jesus in the same winsome, conversational way that he would talk about his favorite team (go, Bulldogs) or his favorite old muscle car. He never missed an opportunity to share his faith.

He gave us the impression that faith in Christ was not something to be ashamed of, but something to be absolutely excited about; and he had an unwritten expectation that we should do the same. Jack loved to say: "Bro, I'm just one beggar showing another beggar where the food is." He did not want us to merely learn about God: he wanted us to be passionate about Him, walk with Him, enjoy Him, talk about Him, and live for Him. His passion was contagious.

Jack wasn't sophisticated, and not everyone took to him, but his wife was. In fact, we could never figure out how he got her to marry him. He would always tell us to "marry up for the Kingdom."

I don't want to paint Jack as the perfect man; he certainly was not a saint. He had a temper that would make an occasional appearance, especially when he was driving. It was always good to see him fight his own demons and watch him struggle to put Jesus first. To this day, when I have some goof pull out in front of me while driving, I say to myself what Jack would say: "Bless his heart," and then for the next block, I try in my heart, like Jack, to actually mean what I just said.

Over time, Jack started collecting a small cadre of high school kids that were making spiritual strides. Fighting was still an ingrained habit I was having a hard time shaking, so my own strides were usually two steps forward and three steps backwards. I was inconsistent, but Jack and Robin were steadfast.

If we do not understand how hard and messy the disciple-making process can be, we can quickly become discouraged. We must be prepared to invest all our heart, time, and energy into the transformations. If we don't have persistence with our disciples, it is like trying to tear open a chrysalis before the butterfly is mature. Sadly, this seems to happen all too often in the disciple-making process.

I read a short brochure of how Napa Valley pioneers turned the raw wilderness into beautiful and productive vineyards. If I am not observant, I will miss all the risk, hard work, patience, and apprehension it took to cultivate their now-multi-billion-dollar enterprises. When I read how missionaries influenced whole countries, if I am not observant, I will miss all the risk, hard work, patience, and apprehension it took those missionaries to achieve their results. It sounds exciting and noble, but if I am not careful, I miss all the commitment, anguish, toil, and time it took for those communities to slowly, begrudgingly, transform.

I am certainly no horticulturist, but if I am not careful, I will also miss the subtleties of Jesus' illustrations that have agrarian emphasis. In contrast, a first-century wine grower would understand exactly what Jesus was talking about when Jesus said: *"'The harvest is plentiful, but the laborers are few; therefore pray earnestly to the Lord of the harvest to send out laborers into his harvest.'"*[58] They knew all about the labor and sweat that went into the creation of a vineyard.

A friend of mine celebrated the birth of each of my children by giving us a young oak sapling. I figured those little saplings would look like giant Redwood trees in no time, but that's simply not the case. My oak trees are not even what I would call mature yet. When I walk through an old forest of oak trees, or an old vineyard, I have a new respect for planters. The agriculturists are long gone, but their legacy lives on!

Jack was my spiritual cultivator. In him, I found a "strength coach" and a "church coach." I had no idea I was part of a 2,000year-old master plan to be one of His workers in God's global harvest.

POSTSCRIPT:

The majority of the people Jesus encountered grew something. The manual labor involved in agrarian life was more time consuming and much harder work (no air-conditioned combine tractors) than it is today. When Jesus would use illustrations like *"The harvest is plentiful, but the laborers are few..."* His audience would clearly recognize the patience and *rugged* work it took to bring crops and livestock to maturity. Also, they would inherently understand that a shortage of labor would result in the crops spoiling. We must never forget that growing things takes time and care. The analogy is plain. *Rugged* spiritual growth takes time and sacrifice.

---

[58] Matthew 9:37, 38.

FOR CONTEMPLATION:

I used to think we were supposed to get people that did not know God into a church, but now I believe we are supposed to help church people get into their community.

- It would be wrong to say that Jesus did not teach His disciples formally. He did, several times; but consider how much informal training was involved to bring the disciples to maturity!
- How ineffective would Jesus' disciples be if Jesus merely said to them, "Let's try and get together in the synagogue every Tuesday for a half-hour?" Jesus walked with His disciples and they not only observed Him but entered into almost every facet of His daily life.
- Our great 21st-century challenge in a compartmentalized post-modern world is finding genuine opportunities for lifeon-life influence. Those opportunities are there, but when they happen, are you intentional about modeling and teaching the truth?

Chapter 8
Rugged Road Trips: Jesus Traveled

"Soon afterward he went on through cities and villages, proclaiming and bringing the good news of the kingdom of God. And the twelve were with him."[59]

Disciple-makers Build Close Relationships on the Road

I am a terrible surfer, but I love surfers! So many surfers I know live a refreshingly *rugged* Christian life. Unfortunately, my skills in riding waves are dismal. My surfing training started not on the fabulous beaches of Australia or southern California, but in a factory behind our old house in Chicago. In the brutal winter months, I would pretend I was riding massive waves while trying to balance on a garbage can lid as I slid down an icy dirt hill. I dreamed of seeing the magnificent surfing beaches I had read about, but never thought I would actually get to surf them.

Christianity has spread around the world, thanks to many radical men and women. Some of these are missionaries who carry surfboards! Surfing ministry has grown so fast, partly because surfers are usually very relational. Over the years, I have become friends with many serious surfers who have patiently tried to help me ride some dangerous waves. Many have been intentional about the Great Commission, and "surfing ministry" has spread to some of the remotest places on the planet.

In Hawaii, while speaking at a Surfing Leadership School, I was introduced as being part of the "Century Club." The Century Club is a group of people who have traveled to more than 100 countries for Kingdom purposes. In retrospect, I never dreamed of becoming a world traveler, but if we are obedient to God's calling, it is incredible where God will take you. I guessed Jesus liked to travel too. He was always saying: *"Follow me."*[60]

As a high school athlete, I embarked on my first spiritual "road trip." Being from a working-class family that lived in a

---

[59] Luke 8:1.
[60] Matthew 4:19.

crazy skydiving world, I had rarely traveled outside Chicagoland, and never dreamed I would actually travel to more than 100 countries. When my friend Jack asked if I wanted to go to Georgia with him, I jumped at the offer. It seems like I have been on the road ever since.

By the end of high school, I had become more involved with Jack, who was my weightlifting coach/youth pastor. By the time I was a senior in high school, he still hadn't been able to get my friends and me involved in his church regularly, but gradually we were making a little spiritual progress.

Jack's passion for Christ was infectious. Many, but not all, of the high school people Jack collected in his ragtag "youth group" were athletes. Many of my friends that came to those first Sunday school meetings on the porch in front of Jack's church drifted away, but my friend Mark (a teammate who had also become a Christian through one of our coach's FCA camps) and I hung in there. One day after a grueling workout, Jack asked us if we wanted to take a spring break trip to his dad's farm in Georgia. Neither Mark nor I had any plans that spring, so we were entirely up for a road trip: anything to get away from the mundane of a Midwest suburb. Thus, a couple days later, we loaded his old pick-up truck, clamped down his rusty camper-cap over the truck bed, and headed south. Jack told us that his dad's farm was old, and although we were going to fish and ride horses, we might need to do a bit of cleaning, and help his dad fix up the old barn. I think Jack had a bit of Tom Sawyer in him. The trip was long and slow. Mark and I rode in the back of the truck on sleeping bags, which I still prefer to being crammed into jets.

When we entered Georgia, I was amazed at how Jack seemed to know everyone. He got coffee and talked to the woman behind the counter with warm and loving ease. Everyone was either his "bro" or "mam." His southern accent did not sound so southern either, compared with the friendly people that we met along the way.

Mark and I were excited, slept little, and talked a lot. As we pulled up to a small, tired-looking gas station somewhere in north Georgia, an old man started filling the tank of Jack's old truck. He peeked into the dirty little window of the cab and saw us. We were sleepy-eyed with matted hair and ratty clothes. He was looking at us with the astonishment of a child peering through the bars of a cage in a zoo.

Jack explained that the two curious creatures in the back of the truck were "nice Yankee boys." Jack said, "Yeah, I was called to do mission work up north." That was his favorite line that always brought a chuckle out of his southern friends. "Yeah, I help pastor a church up in the Chicago area, and these boys are finishing out high school. I am discipling them."

As Mark and I eavesdropped on Jack's conversation with the old gas attendant, we looked at each other a little confused. Did Jack just say that he was discipling us? We thought we were just hanging out with this fun-loving southern guy. I thought, "Well if this is being discipled, I like it!"

> Did Jack just say that he was discipling us? We thought we were just hanging out with this fun-loving southern guy.

When we finally rolled up to Jack's parents' old farm, we were met by a Norman Rockwell impression of what genuine southern hospitality must have been like. Jack's father's name was Papa J, and his mom was called Noni (how is it that the south has all the best names?). Mark, and I weren't sure that we would be accepted. I wondered if Papa J still held a grudge from the Civil War; in fact, I wondered if he fought in the Civil War!

We were soon to understand that this family loved Jesus, and their warmth immediately disarmed us. Mark and I started to realize that Jack had changed and changed a lot! Jack's parents were so proud of him, and grateful that their son, who they hinted was a bit of a "tear-away" in his youth, was now devoted to Jesus.

I had to admit I thought poor Jack's youth ministry had not been going too well. Instead of taking 200 kids to the beach in Daytona for a week, he had decided to take Mark and me to the mountains of Georgia. This, according to me, was not a good career move. We were indeed not "poster" material. No one was going to write about our trip in a Christian youth magazine. We were just two punks looking for a cheap, fun time away from our crazy, dysfunctional lives in the suburbs of Chi-town.

We were immediately immersed in love, and after about an hour, I felt like part of the family, and never wanted to leave.

The conversations about Jesus, horses, fishing, and football flowed naturally on Papa J's farm. Their love for Christ and for others was infectious. Papa J prayed with pure love and reverence. His prayers alone wanted me to get to know God way better than I had before. Watching Papa J and Noni helped me realize that there was way more to marriage and family than I had ever experienced. Also, for years, I had a crush on every southern girl I ever laid eyes on.

We enjoyed working hard on Papa J's farm. I learned he had not fought in the Civil War (which put Mark and me at ease), but he was a former soldier: a sergeant in World War II. It took some prying, but he talked about his time in Germany, and his first encounter with the Jewish death camps. I asked myself: "How could this man, who has seen so much ugliness, still be so loving?"

Not everything was "loving" at that old farm. We learned the horses were not fond of Yankees, or, for that matter, southerners either: but I was determined to learn to ride. Fortunately, I had watched a lot of Westerns. "How hard could it be? All I have to do is sit in the saddle, say 'giddy-up,' and give that ornery critter a good kick in the ribs!"

Mark still loves to tell how I spurred that mean old southern plug with the heels of my dirty gym shoes, and my horse took off like a stampeding water buffalo. I was wondering where the brakes were when my saddle started to slip. Inevitably, I spooked the rest of the horses, and they all began to buck.

Papa J had the meanest horse, which reared up and threw the old sergeant backside-over-frontside! Then my saddle slipped, and off I went, crashing to the ground face first into something soft and smelly. Jack and Mark hung on to their mounts, but I felt so stupid, and was very embarrassed.

There was a bit of chaos, some wild corralling, and finally, we were walking back to the barn. Jack was concerned for Papa J. I was sure they would kick me off the farm for causing trouble, and I was wondering which way was north, and how would I get home by myself. Papa J just rubbed his rear end, looked at me with a smile, and told me, "You did real good, boy. You can really ride!" I felt a bit better.

Papa J scolded the horses—the only time I ever heard him raise his voice—and we sauntered back to the farm. Noni laughed at her husband as he walked stiffly into their little farmhouse. She then fed us a magical southern feast of fried chicken with "all the fixings." The wild horse riders started laughing as all was forgotten. That is to say, except the thousand more times Mark has happily teased me by regaling our friends and my children with an enthusiastic, and perhaps slightly amplified, rendition of the story!

That was the last day we went riding. The rest of the time we worked on the barn, fished, and rode old dirt bikes. Papa J and Jack entertained us with stories about water moccasins, football games, and Jack's wild past drag-racing old junk cars. To our amazement, Papa J had a genuine interest in our young lives. He had a genuine desire to know us: he asked us about our own short history, our sports, families, and our fragile journey with God. He drew out of us stories we had never articulated to ourselves, much less anyone else. He listened to us with sincere interest and enthusiasm, which made us feel valued and meaningful. Georgia was about as far away as I had ever traveled, but it would not be my last trip with Jack. Mark and I (decades later) still talk about that wonderful time on that old farm in the Georgia mountains, and how we were being "discipled" and never knew it.

POSTSCRIPT:

What Can We Learn about Road Trips?

God has used road trips since Adam and Eve were kicked out of paradise. Abraham went searching out the promised land. Moses took the ex-slaves on a forty-year desert trip. Jesus was born on a road trip, and Paul was converted on the road to Damascus. Jesus' disciples have made good use of the road for more than 2,000 years.

A vacation, retreat, or conference is nothing new for a disciple of Christ. When you hit the road, you create a "temporary system." A road trip is a type of short-term parallel universe that takes you out of your everyday routine. God continues to use these temporary systems to help us get to know Him. There are unique dynamics embedded in a trip that jars us out of our old routines and opens our hearts to God.

Throughout the Scriptures, we see Biblical heroes leaving for the wilderness to gain perspective. Moses and the children of Israel must have had the most extensive road trip experience of all time! His people were infected with pagan ideas and practices that God wanted to purge through their time in the desert.

Road trips take you away from the distractions and pressures of ordinary life. Road trips give you more concentrated time together, and they create a platform for more shared experiences. New places heighten your sense of awareness, and help you focus. There's something about getting away which can create openness and willingness to learn.

When traveling, you meet people you may wrongly assume don't like you, and some folks that may openly dislike you. Road trips, when intentional, can create a close, loving community. Traveling and living together generates so many teachable moments that are hard to replicate in a classroom or a coffee shop. Sadly, if we aren't deliberate, the opportunities created by a road trip can be missed.

I used to think disciple-making was best achieved in a classroom, but now I believe some of the best opportunities for discipleship are in an old pickup truck.

As a missionary for 15 years in Europe, I could get cynical about the work that was involved in hosting young American youth from my supporting churches on "short-term mission trips." Kids who, allegedly, came to help us in the summers were sometimes anything but help. Sometimes I would privately add up all the costs for flights incurred to get these short-term missionaries to Europe and consider how I could better spend those funds for Kingdom purposes!

But in retrospect, having kept in touch with many of those American youth (now in their late 20s and early 30s), I am now thankful many are living a *rugged* faith which was fortified by those mission trips. I wished I had encouraged more "short-termers" to get involved! Of course, for many, a flight to Europe is simply prohibitive. I understand that. Our challenge is in developing creative catalytic road trips that are affordable. However, no matter if you are going around the world or across town, it always will take sacrifice.

Just as you may see a school bus go on a field trip, if you were a first-century Jew, it would not be uncommon to see a rabbi walking through your village with his students. In Jesus' day the term "rabbi" was a generic term for "my master." It was a privilege and honor for a rabbi to come and enjoy hospitality in your home and listen to him teach. Jesus loved field trips and seemed to always be on the move. He intentionally took His disciples on the road with Him, and away from their natural surroundings.

On the road, Jesus' disciples experienced hostile crowds, stormy lakes, and enjoyed the hospitality of new friends. They entered into communities and other cultures that the disciples despised. On the road, the disciples watched Jesus take time to get away and pray, to focus, to meet different people, and to listen to His Father.

I think about that *rugged* road trip to Georgia in the back of Jack's pickup truck with fondness. I have never been able to duplicate my first trip to Georgia; God seems always to make things new and fresh. Since then, I have loaded into a lot of planes, trains, tuk-tuks, and motorcycles. I have also brought a lot of young people with me. Sometimes I only have time or resources to take my disciples across the state; sometimes the best we can do is go just across the street; but those magic ingredients embedded in a road trip can help us see God more clearly and bring us closer to Him. Especially when you fall off your horse!

FOR CONTEMPLATION:

- I used to think that travel was a necessary task to get you where you want to go. Now I think that travel is a great tool for being who you want to be.
- Can you remember a trip that was spiritually significant in your spiritual maturity?
- How can you get your disciples away from their usual surroundings this month?
- When you are away, how will you intentionally use your time for spiritual encouragement?

Chapter 9

Rugged Iron: *"One Man Sharpens Another"*

"Iron sharpens iron, and one man sharpens another."[61]

The town was called Mount Pleasant; it was anything but! It was not going well for us as we jogged into the cramped visitors' locker room of Western Michigan University. Their star quarterback's name was Hogaboom, He played ten years in the NFL, and was inducted into the Central Michigan Hall of Fame. We likely contributed to his stardom. Halftime for American football is a short period for a bathroom break, a quick rest, equipment adjustment, and reevaluation of strategy. We didn't get any of those, just very intense yelling. Rarely have I seen a team deteriorate in such a chaotic manner, but our coach seemed to lose his mind, and was screaming, with the aid of all his defensive assistants, and their yelling was concentrated at my friend Russ.

Russ was a starting defensive-back. I have never really understood what those "defensive-back" guys did behind me: he would scare me by yelling at various times in a game, "Watch the crack!" To this day, I am not sure if he was telling me to pull up my pants. However, today it seemed Russ had either committed a high crime or was not playing particularly well.

The coaches found Russ to be the culprit of their losing narrative and took out the season's and their poor coaching on one particular young blond scapegoat. All he could do was scream back at the coaches and teammates, "I can play! I can play!" Russ and I were both from the same high school and were both starting for Northern Illinois as true freshmen. Russ is one of the hardest hitters I have experienced ever, and somehow, he causes pain to those he tackles and those around him, regardless of what team you are on. He had two brothers that played in the NFL, but he was the hardest and most intense player of the bunch. All I could think, as we jogged out of the frenzied locker room was, "Thank God, I am not Russ!"

---

[61] Proverbs 27:17.

I guess Russ' play was not that bad because they never pulled him from the game. We indeed lost, and we at times appeared to lose the plot as well. The bus ride home was dismal. I hated to see what Sunday evening films, where a more sober evaluation was held, would look like for poor Russ. Personally, I thought I had a pretty good game with two and a half sacks on the quarterback.

I was wrong: very, very wrong. Somehow all the woes of our season were deflected off poor Russ and thrown upon poor me.

On closer examination, it seemed the team's loss could solely be blamed, not on the young, blue-eyed boy safety, but on the chubby, brown-eyed nose guard. The film room, like the locker room, erupted into a frenzy of blame, vengeful spite, and malice targeted at none other than me. You would have thought I killed the coach's dog. I now wanted to kill the coach's dog! All the anger that had been pointed towards Russ was now transferred to me. I was the worst player in the football universe; I was an obnoxious residue contrary to all that was good in America; I was the face of illicit insubordination in the eyes of the coaches. I took a quick glance at Russ as my adrenalin spiked, and he was looking a bit sad, if not a bit relieved.

Russ and I had been teammates since high school. He was a great leader, and definitely more spiritually mature than me. Because of the authority of our high school coach, we "towed the line" and steered clear from a lot of things that would inhibit our spiritual growth. We certainly would never curse, but since going to college, my language had started to slip. Since both Russ and I were starting, we were often in close proximity to each other. Whenever he heard me swear, he would slap me in the back of the neck, in the crease between the helmet and shoulder pads, with the speed, authority, and vengeance of the angel Gabriel. He usually would say, "Shut up, Connor." I knew I had blown my witness, and he held me accountable. To this day, if I am hammering a nail in the wall, miss, and hit my finger, and am tempted to curse, I wince and look behind me to see if Russ is there with his righteous justification.

At our awards banquet, freshman year, the coach supplied us with a keg of beer. Our coach was ranting, and talked about going to war with us, I think we would have gone. Russ and I were not drinkers, and we were unfamiliar with the slow mood change as many on the coaching staff and team partook. Our coach was fired the next day.

Russ and I have been friends for over forty years: he is president of the board of directors of the organization I work for and has been a champion of our ministry for decades. Who would have known that he would have such business acumen in his later years? I think he took his intensity in football and transferred it from the locker room to the boardroom. Our first semester of college was frenetic, if not quite academically brilliant. We acquired a new coach who was more of a white tornado, a prince of strictness, insisting on an entirely new level of discipline.

The "first impression" is essential, and my first impression to our new coach did not turn out so well. For our team's first meeting with our new coach (Coach Mallory), he called out anyone who did not meet his and the NCAA's standard of academic excellence. Starting at a 2.0 GPA (grade point average) on a 4-point scale, he started shaming anyone who did not meet the standard. He would call out your name, and you had to stand up. He would then scream out—in abhorrence—your GPA in front of everyone. This was also his first impression of you. After calling out five or six football players, I was shocked that he screamed out, "Russ? Where is Russ!?" Poor Russ stood, his ears turning beet-red. I felt terrible for Russ, but also relieved, thinking, admittedly, I was not as dumb as Russ, so I must have gotten reasonably good grades. Mallory called out a few more names with shockingly bad grades; then it happened. I knew my life as I knew it was over: he called out my name, "Where's Connor, who's Connor?!" I self-consciously stood, and he screamed with all the revulsion he could muster, 0.6 GPA! Now to get a 0.6 GPA, you needed to fail four classes, and get a D in another. I had the worst GPA on the team. Some brilliant collegiate peer told me, "College was great: you did not have to go to class; just read and take the tests!" He was wrong.

It takes a lot to shake the first impression, and that spring was not any better. I had broken up with my girlfriend, was demoted from first string to fourth string, and decided to take a short break from my college, and hitchhike to my friend's college in Iowa. It was nice to get away, but one day slipped into the next, and I missed a day and a half of spring practice. This was unheard of to Coach Mallory, and I was in big trouble. When I finally arrived back on campus, I was summoned to the stadium where most of the team was studying. I immediately lied to my coach, telling him that my car broke down, and there was nothing I could do. My coach was understandably furious: I still have the scars in my ear canals where he chewed me out. Now Coach Mallory's middle name must have been "intense": he yelled at me so loudly and for so long, every player in the stadium heard him: even the toughest players on the team seemed to tremble in the background.

It was going to take a monumental effort to get me eligible to play again. Leaving campus for a day and a half did not help. I needed four A's and a B to transform four F's and a D into an eligible 2.0 GPA (you needed a 2.0 GPA to participate in your sport), and I had just skipped a day and a half of class and practice. Coach Mallory punished me with five weeks of dawn patrol, which means running before school (5:00 a.m.) and spring practice. What really made me popular was that the coaches rotated, and each day, one of the assistants had to get up early to run me.

That night I went to Russ' dorm, where he looked at me like I was the stupidest guy in Illinois. I told him, "Hey I wasn't that dumb: if I had not made up that story, it would have been way worse!" Russ said, "What story?" I repeated the "fib" I told of having my car break down. Russ looked at me like I was a demon, and said, "You lied!" I responded, "No, just a little fib." He answered, "You lied! And you call yourself a Christian! Now go back and tell Coach you lied!" I said, "No way: Coach will kill me!" Russ said, "You lied, Connor! God hates lying!" I meekly responded, "Do I really have to?" "Yes!" said Russ. So, I did, and it changed my life.

Wretched and obsequiously, I walked back to the coach's office, knocked on Coach Mallory's door, and waited. He eventually gestured for me to come in. I was trying to act like I was confident, self-assured body language, chin up, locked jaw, but my words revealed how I really felt. My voice cracked; Mallory's office started to get blurry as I fought back the tears. I tried so hard to be tough. I said, "Coach, I lied. I really didn't break down in my car, I just messed up and left campus, and hitchhiked to a friend's." He exasperatedly looked at me with an impatient expression that said, "You don't think I didn't know you were lying! I have been a collegiate coach for years, and I have heard it all, and you are a terrible liar!" He did not chew me out; he just added two more weeks to my punishment. I was in the most exceptional shape of my life, and ready for the next season.

Russ and I started a Fellowship of Christian Athletes group on campus. Spiritually, I was still taking two steps forward and at times three steps backward. Russ was there to support me in his *rugged* manner. That summer, at the encouragement of our old high school coach (Coach Rex), we became FCA "Huddle Leaders" (Camp Counselors) at a camp in Minnesota.

This was my first experience as a leader (of seven campers), and I loved it. We were well trained, and even during camp, there was time carved out for continued mentoring. I started to realize that summer camp could be, if applied correctly, a "leadership factory." During the FCA camp, I was challenged to give the morning message. I fretted all week, going over and over in my mind what to say with my limited Bible knowledge. I consulted Russ, my high school coach, and other leaders. Finally, the morning arrived, and I spoke. It seemed like I gave a half-hour dissertation, but it actually lasted about 45 seconds. I was exhausted.

The camp was my first foray into formal ministry. I had a taste, and I liked what I tasted. The campers were diverse and loads of fun. My heart started to swell for the youth, and I wanted to see them love Jesus and grow, though I had little clue on how spiritual growth took place.

Going into full-time ministry got into my blood. It was a "calling." After two years of playing football, I decided to give up my scholarship, and find a college where I could study for the ministry. Again, I fearfully walked into Coach Mallory's office. I stumbled with my words, but slowly made him understand that I wanted to go into full-time ministry. He was visibly surprised, but he was terrific, and though he lost a starter on his team, he was happy to give me a letter of recommendation, which he did.

Years later, I would be the chapel coordinator for Coach Mallory, and chaplain to his son's team. He always teased me, saying, "Connor, I'm glad I got rid of you! (like it was his idea for me to go into ministry). You are a much better chaplain than you were a football player!" Coach Mallory and I would meet often. Not long before he died (he still made me nervous), I asked him if he remembered when I came to him and told him that I lied? He got a glint in his eye, was about to say something, thought the better of it, and only said, "I don't remember that stuff; I only remember you were a tough player."

I thank God that I listened to Russ' correction, and returned to apologize to Coach Mallory. Why did I listen and respond to Russ' criticism? I knew somewhere below the intense tough exterior that he loved me. I am grateful to Russ for his *rugged* accountability; the Bible calls it a "rebuke." The church is not so good at that anymore. I can't say I was at the maturity level to "love" the correction: *"Do not rebuke a scoffer, or he will hate you; reprove a wise man, and he will love you."*[62] But now when someone corrects me in love, I am grateful, and my mind goes back to Russ.

If I had never gone to see Coach Mallory and apologized for lying, I would harbor a lie to this day. Jesus said He would *"set you free."*[63] The freedom of repentance gives us a great big world to live in.

POSTSCRIPT:

Show me your friends, and I will show you your future! *"Listen to advice and accept instruction, that you may gain wisdom in the future."*[64] We all need friends in our lives to help us get and stay sharp spiritually. *"Iron sharpens iron, and one man sharpens another."*[65] This proverb suggests we are to be both sharpening and being sharpened. *"Listen to advice and accept instruction, that you may gain wisdom in the future."*[66]

---

[62] Proverbs 9:8.
[63] John 8:31, 32.
[64] Proverbs 19:20.
[65] Proverbs 27:17.
[66] Proverbs 19:20.

My father told me that a dull knife was more dangerous than a sharp knife. Perhaps a dull Christian is more dangerous, too. The book of Revelation is certainly disapproving of lukewarm Christians.[67] No one wants to be spewed out by God, and what has been an antidote for being spiritually dull and lukewarm? To have *rugged* friends.

> My father told me that a dull knife was more dangerous than a sharp knife. Perhaps a dull Christian is more dangerous, too.

That next summer, I cut my teeth in ministry working with a gang (Satan's Disciples) in Chicago. This reinforced in me the idea that your friends will make a massive influence on your life. Most people identify themselves with some sort of group, tribe, family, country, state, school, team, gang, etc. Group identification was deeply entrenched into the first-century culture. Jesus ran a gang, in fact; John the Baptist had a gang; almost all first-century Israelites had a gang. There were Pharisees, Sadducees, Samaritans, Zealots, publicans, tax collectors, scribes, Essenes, Nazarenes, fishermen, Hellenists, slaves, and freedmen. Most gangs were welcomed on Jesus' team (He really liked fishermen), to the shock of the other gangs.

Jesus utilized group learning, and His method was not uncommon from other rabbinical teachers in the first century. Jesus was always being recognized as a rabbi—though Pharisees and Sadducees were unclear where He got his training. *"How is it that this man has learning, when he has never studied?"*[68] Jesus rarely met His disciples one-on-one—He usually taught them as a collective team. Obviously, there was a time concern; training the Twelve would have been considerably longer if His method was purely one-on-one tutorial. Though Jesus' teaching was personal, it was mostly community-based. Why? Because it was effective.

If Jesus had only invited one disciple to hear his Sermon on the Mount, the sole disciple would have little opportunity to be held accountable as he tried to practice what Jesus taught. After

---

[67] Revelation 2:15-17.
[68] John 7:15.

hearing the great list from the Beatitudes[69] and the reciprocal blessings, the disciples had to immediately do their first-century interpretation (hermeneutics) and put those concepts into practice in front of Jesus and the rest of the Twelve. Just as we must wrestle with and live out what it means to be "poor in spirit" in our own "modern" culture, the disciples had to wrestle with and live out being "poor in spirit" in their own culture.

Training in a team creates many dynamics that you can't shape in one-on-one. When the disciples heard Peter answer Jesus when asked, *"But who do you say that I am?"*[70] and Peter gave the reply *"the Messiah,"* that answer would have given the rest of the disciples' courage to proclaim Him at a later date. And if they were anything like me, the disciples may have said to themselves, "I wish it were I who had spoken up and proclaimed Jesus as the Messiah." When the disciples saw that Peter was sternly rebuked and was corrected *("Get behind me, Satan"),* they may have made a mental note not to make the same dumb mistake as poor Peter.

Peer education was a successful model. Rarely did you see the disciples do ministry by themselves. Barnabas understood this when he recruited his old friend Paul to help him with the ministry in Antioch.[71] Paul imitated this model by always bringing individuals or groups with him on missionary trips. Jesus sent out the Twelve and the Seventy-two in pairs.[72] Peer ministry is key to discipleship. I always try to pair up young leaders for our summer camps and outreach events. This helps with accountability, as well as "steel-sharpening-steel" training and support. I have come to see the evangelistic events not merely as an excellent opportunity for effective proclamation, but as leadership training.

Occasionally, I see disciple-makers that are territorial with their young apprentices. Guarding and even isolating them from other groups, perhaps jealous or fearful that they will lose them, or worse, the apprentices will realize that mentor, by comparison, has little left to teach them. This creates a model of

---

[69] Matthew 5:3-12.
[70] Matthew 16:13-20.
[71] Acts 11:25, 26.
[72] Matthew 10:1-20; Luke 10:1-23.

unhealthy jealousy. We should rejoice if we can introduce our disciples to other Christians that are striving to live out their faith. If we can find others that can challenge and take our disciple further than we can, we should celebrate this and understand that we are all part of the body of Christ. Do I enjoy the one-on-one? Absolutely. But watching a group interact and transform into a "steel-sharpening-steel" high-performance team is pure joy.

In peer discipleship, you have young role models, not just old "super saints." In peer discipleship, you have support from people facing the same issues that you do. Many immature potential leaders have resistance to authority, but they may listen and be more open to a peer. In a peer environment, you have a common platform for interaction; friends have a shared interest that will move the culture and create a growing environment.

Most certainly, peer discipleship needs effective and mature visionary leadership to help them stay the course. Without active oversight, peer ministry can go pear-shaped in a hurry. Peter, after the resurrection and before the ascension, went off the rails, left his "fishing for men" commission, and fell back into his old job, while taking six of the disciples with him: *"I'm going fishing."*[73] Jesus again had to set Peter back on course. The combination of peers striving with the help of a strong leader is pure alchemy.[74]

Of course, many of us have been wounded by a person who did not rebuke in love. This keeps us from both being involved in accountability or holding others accountable. It takes discernment and wisdom. Aren't you glad God gave us a book! *"Preach the word; ready in season and out of season; reprove, rebuke, and exhort, with complete patience and teaching."*[75] We are not supposed to rebuke from our opinion. We are also to combine correction with a lot of patience, encouragement, and love. Rebuke is helping others stay on a Biblical course.

---

[73] John 21:1-10.
[74] John 21:15-25.
[75] 2 Timothy 4:2.

75

FOR CONTEMPLATION:

Watching these peer friendships evolve and grow over the years is extremely rewarding. When I meet friends from high school, many are amazed that I have been in ministry for all these years. When I look back at my life, I am surprised, too! I have another particular friend that was part of our high school youth group that has shaped my life with *rugged* love for decades. Do you have someone you trust to speak *rugged* love into your life?

- Is it easy or difficult for you to rebuke a friend?
- What friendships help you to mature spiritually?
- Are you combining correction with a healthy dose of love, encouragement and patience?

Chapter 10
Rugged Providence: *"Rise and Go"*

Providence: the protective care of God... divine guidance...

"Trusting God's providence means that God will use a string of seemingly unrelated events to accomplish His good purpose. We, of necessity, make decisions that seem prudent at the time, but we are completely unaware of how those decisions will play out."[76]

"Now an angel of the Lord said to Philip, 'Rise and go toward the south to the road that goes down from Jerusalem to Gaza.' This is a desert place. And he rose and went."[77]

In college, my friend Mark was so homesick that he started commuting to college. The problem was, it was four states away. His best means of transportation was his thumb. I was amazed— hitchhiking: free travel, stick out your thumb on the side of the road, and wait and see who picks you up. Just like we saw in the old movies, how guys down on their luck were migrating around the United States looking for work during the Great Depression. Mark started the lost art of hitchhiking. It did not take long for his enthusiasm for this cheap form of travel to become contagious. I could hardly wait to get on the road.

The previous summer, I had worked with my dad as an apprentice ironworker during an industrial boom. Sadly, the next year, we were in a severe recession, and there were very few summer job opportunities. I heard that Canada needed forest fire fighters (I thought being a firefighter would help me get in shape for the upcoming season), so I packed my backpack and hitchhiked north. This was at the end of the hitchhiking era; it was rarer to see someone hitchhiking down the road. I packed my

---

[76] Dean Ulrich.
[77] Acts 8:26, 27.

sleeping bag and fishing pole, just in case I had to live off the land. I only fished once on what would be a five-thousand-mile trip that changed my life.

My youth pastor/weight coach, Jack, had taken Mark and me on a few "road trips"; now I was ready to break out on my own. The summer was full of potential. Later that summer, Jack was going to go on a "mission trip," traveling to a Native American reservation in South Dakota. I did not know what a "mission trip" was, but it sounded adventurous.

Mark dropped me off on the north side of Chicago. I reluctantly waved goodbye, quietly wondering to myself if I would see him that evening if this travel scheme became a fiasco. Self-consciously I stuck out my thumb and said a little prayer. Sure enough, a few minutes later, an old car pulled over. I stuck my head in the door and appraised my driver. He seemed kind enough. I jumped in, and sure enough, I was on my way to Wisconsin—no heading back now. Along the journey, I certainly met a few weirdos, and a couple of guys that wanted to hit on me, but the majority of people whom I encountered were very kind and generous. I slept in a field late that night next to a small lake. The next day, after a lot of waiting, and too many short rides and a few detours in Minnesota, I eventually came to the border of Canada. One driver recommended that if I could jump a northbound train, theoretically I would find myself in Canada.

Though I have never read the directions on how to jump a train, there is a right way and a wrong way. I learned not to approach a train from the front of the boxcar. I tried and fell. I can still see those big wheels creaking on the steel tracks. I got up, and picked another boxcar lumbering down the tracks with an open door. This time I approached from the back of the door opening. I grabbed the entry, and let the centrifugal force snap me into the train.

The train was not fast, and that night I slept remarkably well in the unencumbered boxcar. Today, when I am stopped at rail tracks waiting for a train to pass, the tempo of the wheels rolling on the tracks brings me back to that trip. Somewhere in the darkness, I crossed into Canada.

The train eventually stopped early the next morning. I awoke in an expansive railyard. I had no idea where I was. My body was stiff from sleeping on the floorboards. Slowly I got up, packed my sleeping bag, and jumped out into the dew-covered Canadian summer morning. There seemed to be hundreds of trains parked in the railyard. As I was exploring my new surroundings, a guard in a truck rolled up to where I was exploring. I was about to make a run-for it but decided against it. I told the guard my story, wanting to fight forest fires, looking for work, jumping trains. He laughed in his subdued Canadian accent, which gave me a feeling of being far from home. He said with a grin, "Lad, the fires are long out, and besides, you are five hundred miles from where the forest was burning. "So, uh, where am I," I asked. "Winnipeg," responded the guard.

"Where was Winnipeg?" I asked myself. But the guard, seeing my confusion, invited me to his house for breakfast. He was a kind family man, a volleyball coach, and a volleyball Olympic referee. We talked sport, and he tried to explain Canadian Rules Football to me. I stayed the night with him and his family, and on his way to work the next morning, when he dropped me off on the famous highway Canada 1 on the west side of the city, I decided just to keep going west.

When hitchhiking, you experience a contrast between a blast of community with those that give you a lift, then as they drop you off, you experience abrupt solitude as you wait for the next ride. This type of travel taught me something about contemplation and prayer.

Back on the road, my feelings were mixed. I was partly drop-gut scared and lonely, but also somewhat excited for what the future might bring. This has been an all too familiar cycle for me, a contrast between anxiety and excitement about the future. Jesus said not to worry, God is in control: *"Are not two sparrows sold for a penny? And not one of them will fall to the ground apart from your Father."*[78] I am still working on casting out the fear and worry; three steps forward, one step backward. God provided me with a few challenges and some beautiful people on this journey. He still does: His providence is everywhere; we just have to look for it.

> *I am still working on casting out the fear and worry; three steps forward, one step backward.*

---

[78] Matthew 10:29.

A few days later, as the sun was setting, and I was wondering where my next campground/field was going to be, a handsome graduate student with a big smile pulled over to offer me a ride. He told me he was studying for the ministry at some college in Eastern Canada. I still had some old bias towards stuffy Christians. This guy, again, broke those stereotypes with kindness, enthusiasm, and humility. Though I was a lowly vagabond hitchhiker, he treated me as an equal, cared about my welfare, and seemed to enjoy my company. He was going to meet his girlfriend in Calgary the next day at church. The future pastor was exhausted from exams and travel, so he asked me if I wouldn't mind driving for a while. It was a great partnership.

We entered Calgary at night, and I still remember feeling like I was driving into a spectacular lit-up crater. My new friend offered me a couch to "crash on" at his apartment. We went to church the next morning, and he couldn't wait to see his girlfriend. The sermon's focus was from Matthew 6:21, *"For where your treasure is, your heart will also be."* The message was perfect for me to meditate on as I said goodbye to the future pastor and his girlfriend and continued my travel West. I asked myself, "Where is my treasure?"

On the west side of Calgary, I started to hear the news about a major volcanic eruption back in the States. As I continued to make my way west, I was curious if there would be anything to see at the site of the volcano. My geography was not that great, so I was not sure exactly where the mountain was located. They were calling the volcano Mount St. Helens.

Highway 1 in Canada was outstanding, and I was amazed at how many Christians had picked me up. One family, while on vacation, picked me up in their old converted yellow school bus. We rolled along at about forty-five miles an hour. The family and I passed the time by playing cards, singing songs, and playing with their dog. They had no interest or experience in football but were excited to hear that I was also a Christian. Their depth of character and joy was contagious and seemed to flow out of the school bus. Near Vancouver, the bus family said goodbye to me, and presented me with some homemade bologna sandwiches and cookies which I stored in my backpack.

I meandered through Vancouver, and eventually started on my southbound journey. This time, I legally made my way back across the border into the States. I kept a look at my dates, and I wanted to be in South Dakota in a week. I was unconvinced that I would be there on time. Turning from the West to the south in Washington, I perceived a whole new atmosphere. There was a thin haze in the air from the volcanic eruption. The further south I got, the weirder it got. People seemed hesitant and skittish. I learned that I was about to pass (literally) the most earth-shattering volcano eruption in U.S. history. The evidence of ash became more apparent at every mile that I traveled south. The sky was a few shades darker; many were concerned about breathing. No one talked about much else.

I was picked up by one lady in a small pickup truck that lived in a teepee in what she described as a "hippy-commune" with her four kids. I asked what was in the truck-bed. She said, "Manure. Half is for my tomatoes, and half is for my marijuana plants." When we came to Mount St. Helens, the roads bordering it were blocked; the best we could see was from a state roadway off the main highway. It was hard to imagine that over one-quarter of the mountain was missing. Fifty-seven people were killed in its wake. Almost everyone I encountered was a little spooked, and as I kept traveling south, rides were harder to get. There was also a lot more hitchhiking traffic on the roads. There seemed to be a long culture of hitchhikers traveling either south to California, or north to Washington. I was happy to get on the freeway and walk; this certainly is not advised today: that is, unless you want to get arrested. But I was somewhat clean-cut and had a fishing pole sticking out of my backpack, which was an advantage over the hippies that were populating the highway. One guy was hitchhiking in roller-skates. I met another guy that had teardrops tattooed to his face. I learned that each teardrop represented a year in prison.

At another juncture, I met some guys that were dedicated transients. They ask me if I had any money, of which I had little. I realized that in my 2,500-mile trip, so far, I had only spent about $8.75. I was not inclined to give these guys any money, but I did mention that I had a few sandwiches. They looked at the sandwiches that were now three days old, baking in the top of my backpack, and sadly, starting to get ripe. One guy looked at them, laughed, and said, "Hey man, I'm not that hungry." He threw the sandwiches on the road, and another guy, who had been hanging out in a large cul-de-sac, came by and said, "Hey man, don't waste this stuff; I'm that hungry," and greedily carried them away. I kept walking south.

Another mile down the road, I was feeling gloomy as my conscience wrestled over my privileged life, and what the accurate response is to poverty. Across the highway, I saw an old man with a white beard. He was heading north. I yelled across the road, "Are you hungry?" He yelled back in a gravelly voice, "What?" I again hollered, "Are you hungry?" He yelled again, "What?" Finally, I said, "Do you want something to eat?" He made a slight scowl and signaled for me to run across the freeway to talk to him.

I watched for cars and made a sprint to the middle guardrails and then across the road, backpack and fishing pole flopping on my back. The man looked and smelled a bit rough; he seemed to have been living on the road for quite some time. He said to me, "You said you were hungry?" And before I could correct him, he grabbed his cigarettes from his bag, and offered me the remainder, which included some sausage and a few Twinkies. I told him, "Ahh-no, I was asking if you were hungry. Can I buy you a meal?" He smiled and showed me his rotten teeth, shrugged, and said, "That's nice boy, but I'm fine. I'm heading north." We talked for some time, and I was moved that he was going to give me all the food he had. With a melancholy smile, back on the road, thumb in the air, I wondered if I had just met an angel.

Often when you hitchhike, you can get into a rhythm as you build a peculiar rapport with the drivers. I almost always walked backward and smiled at the passing vehicles. I would see slower vehicles pass me, and then I would usually get picked up by a faster-moving car. Finally, we would pass the slower vehicle, and eventually, I would get dropped off and continue down the road. Like the tortoise and the hare, fifteen minutes later, the slower vehicle would catch up and again pass me by. I smiled and waved at the slow-moving vehicle.

This happened often, and one particular motor home in northern California passed me three times over a long hot day. Finally, on the fourth pass, he stopped. A tough old cowboy in his mid-sixties opened the door. He said, "My name is Tom; I have been watching you, and figured if I saw you once more, I might as well pick you up."

Tom told me his story; he had made a small fortune in Alaska in the tire business. Tragically, his family had been killed in a small plane crash two days before Christmas a couple of years earlier. He had sold his business and was "just traveling." Tom tried his best to be a tough guy, but you could see he was in pain. I did my best—as a baby Christian—to share the gospel with him. I was terrified. Why is the greatest news in the world so scary to share? Could it be we are in a spiritual battle? These were some of my first attempts at evangelism. I felt that God had put every person that picked me up there for a reason. Some were much more spiritually mature than I was and had probably picked me up sensing God's calling. Others were not Christians, and I felt it my duty to plant some seeds. It was an excellent education.

Tom and I hit it off, and really enjoyed each other's company. He liked football, but the rodeo was his thing. I think we were both lonely. Tom reluctantly mentioned that he did have a place he needed to be, if ever so briefly. He was a talker, with big stories. Slowly, I came to learn that his entire family was not killed in the plane crash, and Tom was hesitant to explain that he had another son living with a Mexican girl in Reno.

His son had gotten the girl pregnant, and they had a baby. Tom didn't seem sure he wanted to be a grandfather to this couple. The son was a dishwasher for one of the casinos. I got the idea that he and his son were not on good terms. Tom blurted out gracelessly, "My son is not a man's man; we don't have much in common," which made me bristle with sorrow that a father would feel that way towards a son.

He asked me where I was going, and I told him that I was now heading to South Dakota, to meet up with a friend who was bringing some youth from our church to visit a Native American church. Tom told me, "Let's make a quick trip to Reno to see my son, and then I will take you to North Dakota, and maybe I'll even give you my motorhome." It was a strange offer; something did not sit right, but we turned east and headed for Nevada.

Tom and I arrived late in Reno. Tom made a call and arranged to meet his son for breakfast in a casino the next morning. We rolled up to the casino and slept in the parking lot. I learned that Tom's son had rented a place in a trailer-home nearby.

The next morning, as we uneasily seated ourselves around a restaurant table, you could feel the tension. Tom's son and girlfriend, who spoke very little English, both seemed shy. The small family was sweet, and Tom immediately started to warm to them, especially seeing his grandson for the first time. I felt awkward, like an interloper. Halfway through breakfast, I whispered to Tom that I'd better keep going, I waited for him to say, "I'm going with you," but thankfully he didn't. It felt right; I grabbed my backpack out of the motor home, left Tom an evangelistic tract in his little bathroom, and headed to Utah.

Not far out of Reno, I got another lift. We were heading towards the mountains, and I saw a blond-haired hitchhiker holding a sign on the side of the road which said, "Swedish student traveler." I thought that was an ingenious angle for a hitchhiker and was mildly jealous that I didn't have blond hair and a funny accent.

Somewhere in Utah, I was picked up by a really nice man that offered me a place to sleep in his backyard. I pitched my small tent and ate with his prodigious family in their kitchen. We had lively discussions, and slowly I realized that they were Mormons. The next day he dropped me off at the edge of his town and left me with some Mormon tracts. It seemed odd that they were doing a better job of sharing their faith with me than I with them. I had more things to ponder and pray about as I again hit the road, heading to my destination in South Dakota.

Finally, late on a Monday night, I was dropped off in the little town of Mission, South Dakota. It was tiny. In the middle of the crossroad, I saw a policeman sleeping in his car. As I moved closer, I couldn't miss the big revolver sitting on his dashboard. I woke him and he did that jump/gasp thing you do when you realize that you were asleep and did not know it. My voice was shaky as I asked him if he had seen a church group from

Illinois. He looked me up and down while slowly blowing air out of his mouth, like he was Dizzy Gillespie on the trumpet, and gave me a nod. The policeman must have realized I was a bit nervous about waking an officer napping in his squad-car. I think he had been drinking. He understood there were visitors from Chicago who had recently arrived in his town, and he kindly gave me directions. The policeman's acknowledgment sent a wonderful sense of relief that flowed from my head to my feet. Less than a mile later, around one in the morning, I walked through the back of church property to find a bunch of tents neatly erected. I had arrived. My youth pastor/weight coach Jack was dumbfounded to see me. He exclaimed, "How did you find us? It took an hour and a half for us to find this place." They had arrived a few hours earlier; all I missed was setting up of the tents and going to sleep.

The "mission" week provided many more opportunities to share my fledgling faith. These experiences made me realize how pitiful I was at communicating the greatest gift I had. I wanted to do better. The entire journey was seminal to my spiritual maturity. Every step of the way, God had provided people and events to help me grow closer to and love Him more. God also put a few people in my life to encourage on their journey.

My buddy Mark said when I got home, I was a different person.

POSTSCRIPT:

"Now an angel of the Lord said to Philip, 'Rise and go toward the south to the road that goes down from Jerusalem to Gaza.' This is a desert place. And he rose and went. And there was an Ethiopian, a eunuch, a court official of Candace, queen of the Ethiopians, who was in charge of all her treasure. He had come to Jerusalem to worship and was returning, seated in his chariot, and he was reading the prophet Isaiah. And the Spirit said to Philip, 'Go over and join this chariot.' So Philip ran to him and heard him reading Isaiah the prophet and asked, 'Do you understand what you are reading?' And he said, 'How can I, unless someone guides me?' And he invited Philip to come up and sit with him. Now the

passage of the Scripture that he was reading was this: "Like a sheep he was led to the slaughter and like a lamb before its shearer is silent, so he opens not his mouth."[79]

The above passage is a glimpse of how God weaves His providence throughout the world. It's a short chronicle of Philip and the conversion of a trusted leader known only as the Ethiopian Eunuch. It is a cameo of God's daily providence.

The Book of Acts gives us a firsthand view of the expansion of God's church throughout the Roman empire in the first century. Acts help us perceive how God loves His creation and His providential plan for His church. Starting with Jesus' resurrection, and ending with the Apostle Paul's imprisonment in Rome, we see rapid growth. Acts also unpack principles that the early Christians deployed for evangelism and discipleship.

We come to understand that as more people became Christians, the original Apostles were hard-pressed to serve the movement well. Peter asks the emerging group of disciples "to pick seven" to help lead in the work. They were later called "deacons," which merely means servant. The responsibility of the "deacons" went much farther than just serving tables; we read that one of the servant leaders, Stephen, did many *"miraculous deeds and preached with power."* He was our first martyr. Philip, another one of the seven, was later referred to as "the evangelist."

In Acts chapter 8, we read that a "prominent official" identified merely as the Ethiopian Eunuch is sitting on his chariot reading the book of Isaiah. An angel guides Philip on a two-day journey to have an unforeseen, albeit divine, appointment with the African leader.

God provided the great Eunuch with the servant Philip. Phillip found the Ethiopian worshiping God but not fully understanding the implications of the Scripture[80] he was reading. Phillip explained to the Ethiopian the propositions of Isaiah's prophecy, which is made manifest in Jesus Christ. The Eunuch, who had much influence and power, also had a bias for action. He acted quickly to trust Christ for his salvation, and when he saw water, he gladly initiated his baptism.

---

[79] Acts 8:26-32.
[80] Isaiah 53.

"And as they were going along the road they came to some water, and the eunuch said, 'See, here is water! What prevents me from being baptized?' And he commanded the chariot to stop, and they both went down into the water, Philip and the eunuch, and he baptized him."[81]

We find God's provision throughout the Ethiopian's conversion story. The Holy Spirit's prompting, the Word of God, an evangelist to help guide the seeker, a bias for action, as well as a place to get baptized, all by God's providence.

Perhaps with the hindsight of two thousand years, it is easier to see God's historic provision. But He is still working as you read this. Can you recognize it? His providence is as fresh, miraculous, and mysterious as the day Philip found the Ethiopian Eunuch in his chariot. God is employing His Word, the Holy Spirit, His people, as well as a whole bunch of mysterious and sometimes painful circumstances to help you become more of the disciple you were designed to be. He is also weaving your circumstances into the lives of others. God "provides" His love to others through people like you.

> Perhaps with the hindsight of two thousand years, it's easier to see God's historic provisions.

As I hitchhiked around North America the summer after my freshman year of college, I did not appreciate those people I encountered as God's providence in my life. That took a little longer. But as I look back, I see God's divine appointments. He gave me encounters with some beautiful Christians. He put me in front of others that needed a little encouragement, which also led to my *rugged* discipleship.

FOR CONTEMPLATION:

Disciple-making, for the most part, is about long-term, intentional, Christ-impacting relationships. This was God's model to be obeyed by His followers. However, Jesus met many throughout His ministry who would only encounter Him once. He still made an eternal impact on many of those He briefly met.

---

[81] Acts 8:36-38.

87

We should not disregard those unforeseen meetings and serendipitous moments as mere chance. In God's providence, those transitory meetings are making us, and helping others to be made, into His image.

- Looking back at your life, can you remember an example of *rugged* Providence?
- How has God providentially united your life with those you are discipling?
- Are you aware that God may put someone in your life briefly that you can still spiritually encourage? You may never know what an impact you had until you meet in heaven.

Chapter 11
Rugged Rebuke: *"They Will Love You"*

"Let a righteous man strike me—it is a kindness; let him rebuke me—it is oil for my head; let my head not refuse it. Yet my prayer is continually against their evil deeds."[82]

"Do not reprove a scoffer, or he will hate you; reprove a wise man, and he will love you for it."[83]

Summer jobs teach you so many skills which at the time you may not value, but later you may come to appreciate. I admire a roofer's toughness, after a long, hot summer carrying bundles of shingles up steep ladders. I appreciate the skill when watching a woman fell a tree in the perfect spot, missing both the house and the fence, after a summer as a tree-trimmer. I also learned that a *rugged* rebuke while on a balcony trying to paint an old railing is life changing.

One summer before my second year of college, I was hired on as a painter. On a second-floor balcony, I was painting the tenth railing of the day while fighting boredom and trying unsuccessfully to not spill black paint on the poor lady's beautiful roses below me. Whenever I watch a painter ply his craft, hitting the lines and rarely spilling, I am still impressed. That summer, I realized I did not have the temperament or proficiency to be a good painter.

While working for a dubious contractor in a rougher area of Chicago, I was glad to have the company of my friend Mark. Mark has always been an entrepreneur, and he was in the beginning stages of developing what would eventually be a thriving landscape architecture business. Mark was in-between clients, and that summer morning, he was happy for the work. I was grateful for the company—at least for a while.

It was a little annoying, but Mark was always more spiritually mature than I was. He was more disciplined at

---

[82] Psalm 141:5.
[83] Proverbs 9:8.

reading his Bible. Mark had sincere prayers and insights that would often surprise me, and I rarely heard him gossip. He has always been a generous man. My friend Mark was and is the model of trustworthiness and unpretentiousness: he simply has no guile. My wife, to this day, always knows when I am on the phone with him. She says, "No one makes you laugh like Mark."

Mark and I had become Christians in high school at the same sports camp led by our old football coach (Coach Rex). We both played college football at different universities and would come home together for the summers to train. Mark and I were both discipled by Jack, our weight coach/youth pastor. We have had a vital peer discipleship friendship, though I feel I have little to offer him. Mark and I were involved in a lot of crazy exploits together, including sleeping on top of our city's water tower with a cadre of other rascals. He was the best man at my wedding.

Our conversation while painting that morning, drifted from sport to girls to our future plans. And then out of the blue, Mark tells me: "Hey man, you gotta get things right with your dad." That statement stunned and offended me. I immaturely said to myself, "Whose side does he think he's on, my side or my dad's side?"[84] I was referring to the fact that my dad had divorced my mom. He had left my younger sister and me, and he was currently living with a much younger woman—the whole situation was awful.

My whole attitude was quickly souring. I blurted out an expletive and said: "Yeah—right." I stuck my head through the building's balcony, looked across to the next terrace, and I realized he was covered with paint. I said: "Hey man, my dad is a jerk; he should get right with me!" Mark was hesitant: rebuking me did not come easy to him, it wasn't in his nature. He did not wake each morning and wonder whom he should tell off that day. This was painful for him to say. But say it, he did: *"Steve, you need to forgive your dad!"* To which I responded: *"No way! He's a jerk, and he isn't a Christian."* Such a rationalization came quickly to me. Mark went on to emphasize that it didn't matter if my dad was a Christian or not. He told me I had to forgive him, and not forgiving him was

---

[84] I now realize that as Christians, we are supposed to be on "God's side."

ripping me apart. He declared the Biblical truth, that I was to: *"Honor your father and mother."*[85]

When Mark, a dear friend, and a person I loved and respected, said that I had to get things right with my dad, I dismissed him with a curse. I thought: "How dare he open that pain in my life?" My dad was a respected skydiver, but he made his living as an iron worker by walking the beams and erecting steel on some of Chicago's tallest buildings. He was a former alcoholic, and a hard, tough man who loved smoking pot. In addition, my mom was mentally ill, and I watched our small family slowly erode. I thought if anyone understood the pain and shame of divorce, it would be my buddy Mark, as he had gone through the same thing around the same time.

However, Mark's spiritual maturity and theological framework of forgiveness were much more developed than mine. I wasn't in full-blown denial; in principle, I knew forgiveness was not a bad thing; I knew I needed forgiveness all the time. I was simply rationalizing and ignoring the hatred and sin which festered in my soul regarding my father.[86] The antidote for a vibrant Christian life is obedience.[87] Unfortunately, that was something I was to learn slowly, and my intention and execution have always had gaps. I refused to forgive my father. It was an untouchable sin locked up tight in a dark recess of my heart.

My bitterness for my dad became an old acquaintance. The cure seemed more painful than the wound, so I just learned to live with the infectious disease. Over time, it scabs over but never really heals on its own. I walked around terrified that somehow my festering wound would bust open, and I would embarrassingly let out the puss of unconfessed sin. This happened on occasion. Slowly the festering wound becomes part of your identity. I used the hatred to generate anger, which I translated into my sports training and performance. I converted my anger into excuses for an undisciplined life. My unprofessed sin was an anchor to my soul, but my anchor was dredged in a

---

[85] Exodus 20:12.
[86] 1 John 1:8-10.
[87] John 14:21.

91

dark stream.[88] I was pretty good at living the life of a "victim of circumstance."

It took a year of festering. Mark's *rugged* rebuke ("You gotta get things right with your dad") was slowly piercing my hard heart. When wounds fester, they become gangrenous, and paralysis creeps in. I was too angry, too stubborn, and also too hurt to respond to the *rugged* truth.[89]

> There seemed to be a glass ceiling keeping me from blessings and a vibrancy with Jesus that I recognized in other Christians like Mark.

There seemed to be a glass ceiling keeping me from blessings and a vibrancy with Jesus that I recognized in other Christians like Mark. Yet a well-placed, godly-motivated rebuke from a wise man is powerful. Slowly over the next year, I would be confronted by the Holy Spirit. Over time, I became aware that this particular sin was slowly eating at me.[90] As the insightful poet Francis Thomson wrote:

> *"But with unhurrying chase,*
> *And unperturbed pace,*
> *Deliberate speed, majestic instancy,*
> *They beat—and a Voice beat*
> *More instant than the Feet—*
> *"All things betray thee, who betrayest Me."*[91]

Mercifully, God's painful glory was more potent than my willingness to hang on to self-pity. I eventually and reluctantly relented and took my precious hate, a malignant puss, to God and asked forgiveness for harboring bitterness. Somehow it seemed better to take the medicine of forgiveness rather than bear any

---

[88] *I was a dweller by a dark stream*
A crying heart hooked on a dark dream.
In my convicted soul, I saw Your love gleam
And You showed me what you've done
Jesus, thank—Your joyous Son.
Bruce Cockburn.
[89] Ephesians 2:1-5.
[90] Psalm 18:5.
[91] Francis Thompson, "The Hound of Heaven." (G. K. Chesterton called it the greatest poem in modern English.)

longer this particular sin. I asked God to forgive me for harboring such resentment. Over the next year, grace crept into my heart. I began to understand grace, slowly I received grace, and grudgingly I began to give grace. God also gave me some marching orders, but it took a long time to muster the *rugged* courage to respond to God's will.

After football practice on a spring evening, I drove the hour and a half from my university to my father's house for an unannounced visit. You could see my dad's body language stiffen as I came to the door. I was in inner turmoil, knowing what I had to do. Neither Dad, nor his now newly married wife, had anything good to say about Christianity, and to be fair, they had few models of *rugged* faith. They both thought I was just going through a phase and would come to my senses and grow out of it. It was hard to get my dad alone in their tiny house, but I wanted just to have a few minutes to talk.

Before I was a Christian, I had thought to be a Christian was for "wimps and spineless guys." Approaching my dad was the most *rugged* and manliest thing I had ever done. I started with: "Dad, there is something I want to say to you." His shoulders tightened. He set his chin high, and asked: "Yeah, what is it." I was tentative, and through misty eyes, said: "Dad, I-ya, Dad, I-ya, well, I just wanted to say I-love-ya." You should have seen the look on his face. He blurted out: "Are you on drugs?" I said: "No, of course not. It just says in the Bible that I should love you, and I do." He said: "Ahhhh—well, ahhhhh—well, that's cool, Stevie, I-ya, I-love-ya, too."

At that moment, I started to shift from unbridled rebellion to tentative obedience. My heart, like Ezekiel's prophecy, began to soften: *"I will remove from you your heart of stone, and give you a heart of flesh."*[92] The glass ceiling was shattered, and slowly my relationship with God became a little more vibrant.

Please be careful when you hear Christian stories and wonder why your faith is not as vibrant as the person who is telling the story. Storytellers have a tendency to embellish or forget that somewhere between the miracle, there was still a whole lot of anguish and healing that needed to happen. I certainly did not have a perfect relationship with my dad. But slowly, sometimes taking three steps forward, and sadly, two steps backward, I progressed.

---

[92] Ezekiel 36:26.

Some days, old habits would continue to rear up inside of me, self-pity would grab my heart, and I would have to start all over again. My relationship with my dad was not something you would put on a Hallmark card. It was not all jubilation and happiness. Sometimes we still argued. My mom and dad did not get back together. Where there were wounds, there are scars. But slowly, God's grace became "manifest" in me and in my relationship with my old man.[93]

One peaceful day about a year later, I was on the phone with my dad; we were talking, not arguing, just talking father-and-son; it was nice. We talked about skydiving, family, football, and friends. We planned to get together soon. Just before I hung up, I falteringly blurted out: "Ah, Dad, I-ahh-I-ahh-I-ahh-love-ya." To which he falteringly replied: "Hey, Stevie, that's cool, I-ahh, I-ahh-I-ahh-loveya, too." We self-consciously hung up.

Three days later, my dad was dead; while at work, he fell several stories from a building in Chicago. To this day, I thank God for giving me my *rugged* friend Mark the *rugged* courage to provide me with a *rugged* rebuke.

Occasionally I will meet an old man or woman suffused with resentment and slow-burning anger. You can see the sourness in his unrepentant and corrosive spirit, which is slowly killing him. He clings to "the victim" mentality, which becomes a distorted badge of honor. His rock-hard and unforgiving heart has sent him into isolation, a self-imposed exile in a living hell. All I can think is, if it was not for God's grace and Mark's *rugged* rebuke: *"There but for the grace of God, go I."*[94]

POSTSCRIPT:

Reciting the Lord's Prayer[95] is so prevalent in Western culture, we hardly hear it (we even see football teams pray that prayer before competitions). If we are not careful, we can forget that one of the critical elements of that magnificent prayer is forgiveness. A chief principle for our forgiveness is that we are to join in the blessing of forgiving others. I am often taken aback and reminded of my own stubborn heart when I see people who

---

[93] 2 Corinthians 4:11.

[94] John Bradford, English Reformer and martyr.

[95] Matthew 6:5-15.

hang on to hatred and anger in light of how clear Jesus' directive is for forgiveness.[96] In hindsight, I saw that my spiritual walk was encumbered[97] by my willful disobedience by holding onto bitterness. My cure was to *"fix my eyes on Jesus."*[98] My friend, Mark's *rugged* rebuke, was a tough pill to swallow, but God's blueprint for His design[99] always works.

One of my theology professors once told our class that if we were to make up a false religion, we would never publicly embarrass one of our key actors by rebuking him. Yet time and again it is chronicled in the Gospels that Peter (arguably the most central and most outspoken of Jesus' disciples) receives rebukes, seemingly all the time. Peter is a lightning rod for correction. Jesus rescues Peter from drowning, and then says to him: *"O you of little faith, why did you doubt?"*[100] We read that Peter is weakly trying to stop Jesus from His mission in Jerusalem; then Christ harshly tells His beloved Peter: *"Get behind me, Satan!"*[101] After the upper room Passover meal out on the Mount of Olives, Peter is reminded that he will deny his dear Master three times before the night is through.[102]

We watch Peter slowly transform from an impetuous, immature disciple to an articulate, mature leader. The *rugged* rebukes that Peter received were all part of his valuable disciple-making education and were a great fulfillment of a great Old Testament verse: *"It is better for a man to hear the rebuke of the wise than to hear the song of fools."*[103]

My father's early death still casts a long shadow over my life. It makes me more grateful for friends like Mark, who are persistent and loyal. He makes a conscious effort to encourage his disciples, and he is also very patient.[104] Mark wisely did not blast me after his rebuke with righteous indignation; he just loved me and let the *rugged* truth simmer in my heart. I have watched Mark over the years, and I realize that he is excellent

---

[96] John 6:14, 15.
[97] Hebrews 12:1, 2.
[98] Hebrews 12:1, 2.
[99] Genesis 1:26.
[100] Matthew 14:31.
[101] Mark 8:33; Matthew 16:23.
[102] Matthew 26:34.
[103] Ecclesiastes 7:5.
[104] 2 Timothy 4:2.

at a slow, gentle pursuit. Mark and I have continued to be friends. In college, we agreed to a fifty-year study together on the Bible verses from Romans 12:1, 2. Our research has given us decades of great insights and satisfaction.

FOR CONTEMPLATION:

Many of my closest friends are those that I have discipled or been discipled by. We have maintained a *rugged* friendship. I have on those rare occasions rebuked some of my disciples. I don't find it a pleasant thing to do. Most of these men have taken my Biblical instruction, and happily applied it to their life. Sadly, a few have become resentful, and walked out the door. Sometimes they come back with a new appreciation for *rugged* Biblical guidance, and actually thank me for speaking truth into their lives. The others? Well, a gentle pursuit. Scripture tells us there are significant benefits for receiving a *rugged* rebuke from a godly person, and some rough consequences when you don't heed Biblical instruction:

The Benefits of Heeding a Rebuke

- Honor (Proverbs 13:18)
- Prudence (Proverbs 15:5)
- Intelligence (Proverbs 15:32)
- Knowledge (Proverbs 15:32)
- Interaction with wise people (Proverbs 15:31)
- Staying on the path of life (Proverbs 10:17)
- Being Spirit-filled (Proverbs 1:23)

The Consequences of Not Heeding a Rebuke

- Stupidity (Proverbs 10:17)
- Foolishness (Proverbs 12:1)
- Self-loathing (Proverbs 15:32)
- Poverty and disgrace (Proverbs 13:18)
- Death (Proverbs 15:10)
    - Can you remember a time in your life that a certain rebuke was important to your spiritual maturity?
    - What is the best attitude to have when you rebuke those you are discipling?

- What would have happened to the disciples if Jesus had not on occasion rebuked them?

Chapter 12
Rugged Character: Finding Our Identity

"For this very reason, make every effort to supplement your faith with virtue, and virtue with knowledge, and knowledge with self-control, and self-control with steadfastness, and steadfastness with godliness, and godliness with brotherly affection, and brotherly affection with love. For if these qualities are yours and are increasing, they keep you from being ineffective or unfruitful in the knowledge of our Lord Jesus Christ."[105]

"For while bodily training is of some value, godliness is of value in every way, as it holds promise for the present life and also for life to come."[106]

"The Christian alternative to immoral behaviors is not a new list of moral behaviors. It is the triumphant power and transformation of the Holy Spirit through faith in Jesus Christ—our Savior, our Lord, our Treasure."[107]

A Man of Character

Our Lord gave me an unusual and specific marching order while I was lying face to the floor, praying. A wave of gratitude had come over me while praying, and I felt an uncontrollable urge to start thanking God for all the fantastic people that have discipled me. Soon I was thinking about my years in southern California, and of course, Coach Terry.

While praying, I had one of those rare lucid moments with God. He told me I was to get off my face and do something. I was to call Coach Terry, and, on behalf of all us athletes, thank him for the massive influence he had had on all us. Coach Terry was now actually "Dean Terry," the Dean of Students for a large Christian university. He was a busy man, and it often took a few

---

[105] 2 Peter 1:5-8.
[106] 1 Timothy 4:8.
[107] John Piper.

days for him to get back to me. Imagine my excitement when Terry took my call on the first ring.

Listening to his voice, which is almost always bright and cheerful, he uncharacteristically sounded tired, like a broken bell. I told Terry: "Hey Coach, I know this is outta-the-blue, but I was praying, and the Holy Spirit told me to call you, and on behalf of all those students, I am to thank you for the incredible influence you have had on us." He started to cry.

Back in college (decades earlier) at the start of my junior (third) year, I was lacking direction. I loved playing football, but academically, the classes were uninspiring. All I really wanted to do was study the Bible and learn how to become a pastor. I was smart enough to know I didn't have a clue how to do it.

After two years of lettering on a Division 1 football team, I was still dissatisfied with life, and struggling for direction. After experiencing a short-term mission, and being a counselor at various Christian sports camps, the only thing I really wanted to do was help others know about Jesus. I also knew that I had a lot of growing up to do (I still do), and I needed to learn the Bible.

With fear and trepidation, I went into my coach's office, and let Coach Mallory know I was leaving our team, university, and full-ride scholarship. I awkwardly tried to explain my dilemma. He was initially perplexed, "You? You want to go into ministry? You?" I thought he would chew me out, but instead, he offered me some game film and a letter of recommendation. Years later, I would serve him and his team (and years later, his son's team) as their sports chaplain. He would laugh and say: "Connor, I'm glad I got rid of you!" (Like it was his idea!) "You're a much better chaplain than you were a football player!"

That next semester, I searched for the best college, and volunteered in several ministry positions. I missed my teammates, but I did feel liberated. It was one of the first autumns in my life that I wasn't focused on beating an opponent. However, I hadn't a clue about what was next!

As I was searching for direction, Jack, my old high school weight coach/youth pastor, invited me to his church to listen to a speaker who was giving a series of lectures/sermons.

After the talk, Jack asked several college students back to his house for an informal question and answer session with the speaker. My friend Mark and I were virtually inseparable at this time, and he asked Jack's friend: "If you were going to go to college today to become a youth pastor, where would you go?" He immediately suggested a university in southern California. That sounded interesting and filled my imagination with all sorts of exciting adventures. I enrolled and hitchhiked to southern California after Christmas. They even had a football team.

Southern California would be my first experience in culture shock. Soon after my arrival, I met Coach Terry on the campus tennis court. Terry was an assistant football coach, and head track and field coach. He was teaching a PE class, and trying to train some of his Nigerian track stars how to play the game; there was a lot of laughing going on.

Coming from a Division 1 university to a lowly NAIA Christian college, I was trying my best not to be big-headed. Any cockiness I might have had was soon wiped away when I walked onto the tennis court. I was immediately humbled by some incredible physical specimens: some of the greatest athletes in the world were in Coach Terry's class, trying to learn how to play tennis. Evidently, Coach Terry could recruit.

Terry and his wife Nancy both looked like they could have gone down the road to Hollywood and been movie stars. Terry was a *rugged*, handsome man; he looked like he could still crush a linebacker, and he was quick with a kind smile. Wherever he went, students hung on him. His old southern California office looked like a shoe box packed with sports gear and papers to grade. It featured a rusty filing cabinet festooned with track and field advertising stickers and stuffed with track and field stuff. His tiny office mostly overflowed with students that needed encouraging, or just seemed to love hanging around Coach Terry. What really attracted students to him was his loving and humble character; Christians call this godliness. I started hanging around Coach Terry, too.

Terry would eventually be inducted into the NAIA Track and Field Coaching Hall of Fame. He has coached many world-class athletes, but his real legacy has been all the students he continues to disciple. His motive came out of his love for God.

Terry kept drinking the "living water," and it was out of that deep well that his heart flowed with a deep love for thirsty college underclassmen.

In my senior year, I had a dream of creating an outreach that would engage the university athletes with local youth pastors. We called it *Night of Champions*. At the time, my organizational skills were wanting; I couldn't administrate myself out of a paper bag. Fortunately, Coach Terry and his wife Nancy were there for me. "Hey, Coach, do we have a budget for hamburgers and hot dogs?" "Hey, Coach, I need a gym; can you arrange that, please?" "Hey, Coach, can you bring your BBQ grill?" "Hey, Coach, did I mention that you are the MC of the event?" Coach Terry would give a wry grin, and say: "What next, Conman?" I said: "Can we borrow your truck?"

The *Night of Champions* was a terrific event; it affirmed in my heart that ministry was my calling. Terry would continue to build the *Night of Champions*, and it has taken on a life of its own. Thirty years later, it has become one of southern California's most significant annual youth events, and an excellent tool for regional youth pastors. Thousands have committed their lives to Christ, thanks to Terry and Nancy's commitment to evangelism.

Coach Terry was not just generous with his BBQ grill; he was generous with his life. Terry had every "worldly" right to walk around with a haughty demeanor. He had a beautiful family; he was a great athlete, an accomplished coach and administrator; but he remained humble, and never took himself too seriously. I would hear him say: "Conman, I have been working on my outer man for years. I want to make sure I am working on the inner man." When he spoke of wanting to love his wife and family more, it made me want to love my wife and family more. When he spoke of giving more financially, it made me want to give more of my finances. When he spoke of needing more humility, I was shocked. How could this man be more humble? It shames me (in a healthy way) to live a humbler, Christlike life. Terry's desire to build his character to be more like Jesus' character (godliness)

> "Conman, I have been working on my outer man for years. I want to make sure I am working on the inner man."

made me desire to be more like Jesus. Both Jesus' and Terry's character are contagious.

You don't bring a knife to a gunfight. If we are to take the Great Commission seriously, we must bring the best weapons we can to the fight. There were many professors and pastors I tried to get to know, but they would rarely let you actually see their lives. They could teach theory, but they had trouble modeling the truth they pontificated. One of the Apostle Paul's most powerful tools was transparency, his willingness to allow us to watch him struggle to become a more godly man. When I have been open with the men I have discipled that pornography has been a challenge, they almost always thank me for my candidness. They often exclaim, "I thought that I was only one who had that challenge."

So, back to praying in my office years later: I felt the prompting of the Holy Spirit to call Coach Terry and thank him for what he meant to all of us knucklehead students he had discipled. I did, and his tears flowed. This was the first and only time I have heard him cry.

I found out he was visiting his hometown in the Bay Area. He was exhausted and feeling uncharacteristically blue. A family member was dying, and he was there to encourage them. He decided to go for a walk on a favorite old running trail near the San Mateo Bridge—a place he had frequently run when he was a high school and college athlete. He had gone to pray and look for answers. Terry was drained, and uncharacteristically asking God and himself whether he was really living a useful life. This was not the first time he was on that trail looking for answers.

Decades earlier, some of Terry's college football teammates started sharing their faith with him. He really respected the student athletes and gave them a few minutes of their time. As an unchurched college student, he was not sure he wanted to commit his life to God, but then he started to feel a transcendent grappling in his heart, and he couldn't shake what he later understood to be God's calling. Terry wanted to fight it and kept saying to himself: "I just need a little proof." Like any athlete trying to escape from God, he ran – literally! He went for a run. A shirtless, all-hulked-up student-athlete trying to outrun God. He couldn't shake Him.

Finally, he came to a crossroads. Should he continue his wild selfish life, or totally surrender it to Christ? He stopped on that *rugged* path, and asked God for a sign. "Hey, God, are You there? If so, then show me!" Another example of being careful what you pray for!

Immediately a small shorebird (killdeer) mysteriously flew around his head in a tight, concentric circle. Terry was a little stunned. He asked: "Hey, God, did I miss it? Was that bird Your sign? If so, have the bird do it again!" Immediately, for the second and last time in his life, the little killdeer again circled his head. A few days later, in the Oakland Coliseum, Terry committed his life to Christ at a Billy Graham event.

Back to the tearful phone call...

"Hey, Coach, what's going on? Are you okay?"

"Conman, this is uncanny. God gave me a sign almost forty years ago—at this same place. Now, today you tell me God told you to call me right when I'm on this exact same spot!" He went on to describe his conversion on that *rugged* path, and how he was at that very moment looking for a little encouragement, a little affirmation. He was asking: "Was my life useful?" He went on to say: "Conman, on the same exact place that goofy bird flew around my head, God tells you, one of my goofy students, to call me, out of the blue, all the way from Indiana."

Coach Terry is a man of character, and always on a mission to be more like Christ. Does our life reflect Christ's nature? Do the people we are influencing want to imitate our character? Do they understand the struggling it takes for us to become more Christlike? Do we recognize the building blocks of character? If we do not really know that we were made in the image of God, we will have trouble building our character, and building into the lives of the people we are discipling.

Losing Our Identity

Almost every culture values character. Yet, if it is so valued, why is it so hard to find and develop? My old colleague Stuart loves to say: "Sin breaks everything." It breaks our love, our faith, and our hope. All have been shattered by sin. I find when I have in-depth, spiritual, and theological questions, I find the answers in Genesis 1-3. God told us we were created in the image of God. This is foundational to character. At the Fall in the Garden of Eden (when sin entered the world), our image was shattered, and like Humpty Dumpty, all the King's men couldn't put us back together again. At the "Fall of man," we lost our identity. Humans have been trying to interpret their species since. Fortunately, God has given us a blueprint for His human design.

The Menagerie

We all have fears growing up. Some fears are valid, but many are imagined. As a child, I watched the training films of how not be vaporized by an atomic bomb. The answer was to hide under my desk! I thought if I was on the playground when the bomb hit, I was a goner. The flying monkeys in the "Wizard of Oz" movie caused me some worry, but I was a chubby kid, and very much doubted they were strong enough to carry me away. My dreams of being an astronaut (as a five-year-old) were dashed by watching reruns of the old Star Trek television show—the real old one.

One particular Star Trek show still puts "heebie-jeebies" up my spine. The episode was titled "The Menagerie." The main plot was about a desperate alien-life form from a planet called Talos IV. The aliens were called "Talosians," and they had ruined their population and environment.

The Talosians were now trying to repopulate their planet by luring humanoids to mate. Ah-ha, I didn't know what that meant as a little squeaker either. They had captured and paired a very able Captain Pike (who had been hideously injured) with Vina, a female who had previously crash-landed on Talos as a baby.

What really scared me was the subplot. Vina, who was severely mangled, and the only survivor of a crash into Talos IV, was "reassembled" by the Talosians. Unfortunately, the near-extinct Talosians did not have a blueprint for human design. Not having a prototype, the Talosians rebuilt her in a shape that was very different and quite deformed from her original form.

Somehow as a young boy, that particular story filled me with dread. At that time, I did not know I was made in the Image of God.

I was taught that I came from a primordial soup. Maybe that is why I don't like soup. No one ever told me I was created by God, and that *"I am fearfully and wonderfully made."*[108]

The Talosians eventually realized that they had reassembled Vina in a frighteningly hideous form. They had no blueprint to follow. To rectify their mistake, they put her in their "Reality Distortion Field," which locked her into a cage of false existence. We later learn that the Reality Distortion Field was the very thing that was destroying the Talosian species.

The real fear for me as a young and hopeful astronaut was crashing into an alien planet, and also being put back together in a similarly shocking form. I imagined flying back home and trying to explain to my mom why my leg was growing out of my head. By the end of the show, it dawned on me that being an astronaut might not be my calling.

If we are to respond to the Great Commission, we need to understand the foundational building blocks of God's design. If we don't understand the design, we won't be much use as disciple-makers. If our job as disciple-makers (to produce, reproducing reproducers) is to help another soul to become mature in Christ, then we better have and use the blueprint (image of God), and know what a human was originally designed for, and what we looked like.[109]

POSTSCRIPT:

Sadly, ask any twenty people what character means, and you may get twenty answers. Ask twenty pastors what the difference between "character" and "integrity" is, and you most certainly will muddy the waters.

Character is classically meant as virtue. The etymology (origin) of virtue merely means "man" in his purest function and original design. Seven classically agreed virtues that are associated with mankind are: prudence, temperance, justice, courage, faith, hope, and love. The first four of these are philosophical in nature. The latter three are theological in nature.

---

[108] Psalm 139:14.
[109] I thank CSRM for popularizing the phrase "to produce, reproducing, reproducers."

Integrity is the degree to which humans utilize each of these virtues. The root word of integrity means whole or complete.

Jesus, as a sinless man, modeled all of these virtues. Our job as disciple-makers is to recognize and develop each virtue/characteristic in our own lives and encourage them in the lives around us. How do we build character? The Apostle Paul explains we are transformed by the renewal of our mind, to allow God's truth to flow through us, and allow the power of the Holy Spirit to constantly shape us.[110]

I spent years at Oxford University (Pastorate), and to my astonishment, I would get roped into sitting on debate panels. Here I was, the dumbest guy in the room, trying to defend the foundations of the universe. Of course, at first, I was terrified, but it did occur to me that though everyone in the lectorate might be smarter than I, I had the truth. We all know what the truth does for you: it "will set you free"![111]

In one panel, a brilliant woman and formidable debater mentioned that she had experienced throughout her life a "large measure of autonomy." She stated that if she found herself in a position that life was not worth living, she felt she had every right to "Die with Dignity." By this, she meant euthanasia. It is hard to argue with a person that is adrift in the popular notion that we can arbitrarily invent values we deem convenient for a particular set of circumstances.

I agreed with her that I also thought it would be wonderful to die with dignity. I did say that her version and my version of "dignity" could not be further apart. If you don't ground your life in God's basic building blocks for the human being (truth), you will become unmoored from reality.

Our Character Is Not Arbitrary

As part of a team of writers in South Africa for a sports ministry alliance, I was wrestling through the principles of character. The group was working on a program to help coaches, at all levels of sport, develop a character development curriculum. By the time the World Cup came to Africa, the alliance had trained over thirty thousand coaches.

---

[110] Romans 12:2.
[111] John 8:31, 32.

At a writing session, one Western leader said to the team that he had picked a few fundamental "values" for his family. He chooses individual "values," and reinforced them in a contract. Another writer said: "That sounds all well and good, but you are approaching it wrongly. You are taking a secular tactic (pick and choose values/character that may seem right for you) and trying to make it a Christian policy." She went on to say: "We don't get to select our values. If God made values, we must embrace them—all of them. We do not get to pick and choose."[112]

What the writer was saying is that we do not get to cherry-pick certain truths. That is like a person that decides to have healthy hygiene, and chooses to shower, wash his hair, trim his nails, but chooses not to brush his teeth.

> *What the writer was saying is that we do not get to cherry-pick certain truths.*

We don't get to pick and choose the foundational building blocks that seem convenient. God has given us the building blocks of humanity (character). We must realize that these "values" are, to some degree, broken in our lives, and we are to enter into a relational pact with God to have Him repair our character. The Declaration of Independence says, *"We hold these Truths to be self-evident."* It does not say, "Pick and choose arbitrary truth that makes you feel good."

FOR CONTEMPLATION:

What I love about Coach Terry is that he is always working on the inner man. He understands he has purpose and wants to be the best for his Master. This is challenging and attractive. After talking to Coach Terry, I often, with more clarity of purpose, ask myself, "How can I best respond to the Great Commission by working on the inner man?"

Keep asking:

- What are the blind spots in my character?
- How do I find them and work on them?
- How can I encourage others to be transformed and reflect on being "the image of God"?

---

[112] Character Curriculum session, Sports Movement, South Africa, 2009.

Chapter 13
Rugged Warrior: "Go Out to Fight"

So Moses said to Joshua, "Choose for us men, and go out and fight with Amalek. Tomorrow I will stand on the top of the hill with the staff of God in my hand."[113]

"Thank God for the battle verses in the Bible. We go into the unknown every day of our lives, and especially every Monday morning, for the week is sure to be a battlefield, outwardly and inwardly in the unseen life of the Spirit, which is often by far the sternest battlefield for souls. Either way, the Lord your God goes before you; He shall fight for you!"[114]

We don't put on the "Armor of God" for a photo-op, but rather, we were given these tools for battle! The Apostle Paul loves the warrior themes to help explain the meaning of life. In most walks of life, you will find *rugged* Christians employing the most powerful weapons at hand: love, truth, righteousness, the gospel, faith, salvation, the Word of God, prayer in the Spirit. The scope of our spiritual warfare is with the world, our flesh, and the devil.

My first afternoon on the Chicago Bears campus as a rookie free agent, I tried my best to act like a veteran player. I didn't want to reveal my true emotions, which were a mix of apprehension and a dizzy thrill of being surrounded by many of my heroes that I had idolized since I was in the seventh grade. Part of me just wanted to run around the locker room and ask everyone for their autograph. As the season ended, I was part of a historic team, arguably one of the best defenses in the history of the NFL. We certainly had some of the biggest characters in Chicago Bears history.

Among the team were a few *rugged* Christians. I sat down for a team meeting next to a defensive back named Les. I had read a magazine article about Les that claimed he was a Christian.

---

[113] Exodus 17:9.
[114] Amy Carmichael.

When I got the chance, I whispered in his ear a little apprehensively: "Hey, Les, I heard you're ... a-ahhh ... you're involved with a Bible study?" He whispered back: "Hey brother, speak up, man—speak up!" I whispered again: "I heard you speak at several churches." He again whispered: "What did you say? Speak up, man, speak up." I responded even more quietly: "Hey Les, I heard you are a Christian?" He jumped right up in front of the whole team, grabbed my arm, and yelled: "Hey, Jim McMahon. Look out, we got another Christian on our team!" I was a little taken aback, to say the least, but a sense of courage filled me, knowing I was in the presence of a man that was not intimidated at being a Christian.

There's an old saying: "Sport may not build character, but it certainly reveals it." A professional football team is a collection of eclectic athletes snapped up from several varied backgrounds and mind-sets. You have a range of attitudes from anti-God types to *rugged* outspoken Christians. A locker room can be an excellent opportunity to let God work through you; it is also a battleground, and our most potent weapon is *rugged* love. My colleague and friend Greg Linville claims the Apostle Paul was trained in the gymnasium alongside the Cydnus River of Tarsus, and that makes sense to me because I've always thought the Apostle Paul would jump at the opportunity of being on a sports team.[115] All I know is it would be inspiring to watch him live out his faith in the sundry atmosphere of a professional football team. Of course, I didn't get to see the Apostle Paul, but I did get to see some authentic *rugged* professional athletes who took me under their wing that lived by the words Paul was inspired to write.

Les next asked me. "So, what's your verse?" I asked: "My verse?" "Yeah, man, all us Christians on the Bears sign our autographs with a verse. We put it at the end of our name to encourage folks to read the Bible. So what's yours?"

Wow, I didn't have a "verse!" but I wanted to get one fast!

Most things in my Christian life happen slowly, or at least slower than I want! I knew if I picked randomly through the Bible and came up with *"[Judas] went and hanged himself!"*[116] it would be counterproductive.

---

[115] Greg Linville, *Christmanship*, p. 200.
[116] Matthew 27:5.

It took a while, but after some prayer, the verse that kept coming back to me was: *"The thief comes only to steal and kill and destroy. I [Jesus] came that they may have life and have it abundantly."*[117]

This verse connected with me because my father was a skydiver (he once held a world record), and I observed how he lived an exciting life, in many ways pushing the envelope. So, even though I was a relatively young Christian, I knew I wanted to live full-out for Christ. Thus, my verse was John 10:10, and it resonated with my young warrior and adventurous heart. Have life to the "full!" Life to the max, seven days a week! Be a max-seven-man! That's what I wanted; that's what I saw in many of my teammates. Several players encouraged my faith during that time, and many remain my friends.

Years later, on the sideline of Penn State vs. my Indiana University team, I felt my pocket buzzing. Over the years, I have been a chaplain for several teams, and I was currently working as a chaplain for Indiana University football. I knew it would look silly during the heat of a televised college game for one of the staff to be talking on his mobile phone. It would be a perfect "gotcha" television clip! Yet I knew who was calling me, and I did not want to miss him. He had been calling me for years. So, I slipped into the locker room and answered my phone. It was my friend and former NFL All-Pro Norm wishing me a happy birthday. Norm has been calling me since he knew me as a rookie free agent with the Chicago Bears.

Norm's remarkable NFL career spanned 14 years and was highlighted by: playing on the only undefeated season for the Miami Dolphins; competing in three Super Bowls; and winning two! More importantly, he is a Sports Ministry pioneer. What may seem common for us today (athletes giving public testimonies for Jesus; Sports Chaplaincy for high school, college and professional teams; pastoral care for athletes and their families; and thousands of local churches engaged in Sports Outreach Ministries), Norm and other *rugged* warriors bravely pioneered.

After he retired from the National Football League, Norm and his wife Bobbe established a ministry for professional and former professional athletes. For decades they have traveled the

---

[117] John 10:10.

110

continent and the world, discipling athletes and their families. As a player, he visited the Bears' training camp. Though I was a free agent, he treated me as if I was a star. He had nothing to prove as an athlete and cared little about how much playing time you got, or whether you were making an impact on the team. That was good for me because I was doing neither.

Norm and Bobbe have sustained a long ministry with several high-profile athletes, families, and extended families. A key to their discipleship is evangelism. They are not afraid to share their faith and hold accountable those they disciple to also boldly present the gospel. Norm is a *rugged* warrior and has often said: "The church does too much leadership training, and not enough leadership doing. I want to see an army of Christians in the world of sport!"

Norm and Bobbe have held conferences for professional athletes in various sports for years. A vital part of their ministry is training young athletes to clearly and effectively proclaim the gospel, one-on-one, as well as in big events. The Evans don't just teach; they actually send out their athletes out to share their faith. The hallmark of their ministry is: "Not just *training* but *doing*." Norm has told me several times over the years: "Man, we are in spiritual warfare, and we need to prepare our people for battle."

Norm simply and humbly models Jesus' ministry. Jesus' training of His twelve disciples included evangelism. Jesus later expanded His evangelism from twelve to seventy-two.[118] Part of Jesus' master plan to reach the world was to prepare the disciples to make disciples by sending them out to do spiritual battle. You never learn to climb a mountain by walking around it. Do you ever see Jesus happier than when His disciples return from their season of ministry: "In that same hour he rejoiced in the Holy Spirit and said, 'I thank you, Father...'"?[119]

The lesson of "more leadership *doing*" has stuck with me through the years. In a global conference in Thailand, I was asked to facilitate the formation of all the North American churches and organizations gathered to do strategic planning. We asked ourselves: "What can we do together and for the Kingdom that we

---

[118] Luke 10:1-23.
[119] Luke 10:21.

can't do on our own?" In one of the first meetings, I was supposed to do an experiential-learning icebreaker. Icebreakers are good ways to catalyze new friendships and drop personal agendas for a bigger picture.

Some of the icebreakers utilize silly games, which I find a bit contrived. I took a page from Norm's playbook (which he received from the Bible) and gathered the seventy-plus leaders together. I explained that the next hour and a half was set aside for an experiential learning exercise. I asked the leaders to pair up with someone they didn't know. I then said: "Instead of some silly game in our conference room that simulates ministry, I want you to go out into Thailand with your new partner and do evangelism." A few laughed like I was joking. I said, "We will meet in an hour and a half to see how it goes." We prayed and dispersed. Many of the leaders brightened at the thought of getting out of the stuffy hotel, and actually doing ministry. What shocked me was, about one-third of my North American leaders did not leave the lobby of the hotel! One chap said to me, "I just couldn't look at the prostitutes as they had drinks with westerners." I was so frustrated that these "leaders" were unwilling to be "doers." Many who were well paid to create policies for their respective ministries—were all talk.

I was lamenting to Norm about the one-third that remained in the lobby. He smiled with that big Texas grin, and merely said: "Now, you know which leaders to work with."

> *"Now, you know which leaders to work with."*

When Michelle and I became missionaries in the United Kingdom to help pioneer sports ministry there, Norm and Bobbe came to encourage us three years in a row. They invited Michelle and me to several professional athletes' conferences for us to either just rest or to do training. The Evans have discipled several *rugged* athletes who became great leaders in their communities, churches, and around the world. I have seen them at the end of a season of ministry tired and spent, but very satisfied. Norm was a *rugged* warrior on the playing field, but more impressive, he is an adroit cosmic warrior for Christ.

POSTSCRIPT:

We have had several *rugged* warriors in Biblical history. One of my favorites is Joshua, who, at the end of his long career, challenges his people: *"Choose this day whom you will serve... But as for me and my house, we will serve the LORD."*[120]

Joshua was discipled by Moses, and eventually, the mantle of leadership passed to him. It is a rare and exemplary transition of ascendancy from one great leader to another. This is a model of leadership that we disciple-makers should examine carefully.

One of the first things that Moses did was to empower Joshua, and send him to battle as the leader against the formidable Amalekite combatants.[121] While Joshua fought, Moses stood on a hill and held his famous "staff of God" high in the air, on a mountain, as a representational act of prayer. In a tender scene, we watch the aged Moses struggling to keep the staff overhead. When the staff was lowered, Joshua's army faltered; when the staff was propped up, with help from Moses' top advisors Aaron and Hur, Joshua triumphed. Joshua beat the Amalekites.

The *rugged* warrior not only won a strategic battle, but he quickly learned a critical lesson, a lesson that would carry on throughout his successful career. Joshua learned that his sufficiency was not in the power of his might, but in the power of God.

That night Joshua was able to lay his head down on his pillow (or whatever former Egyptian slaves, and now nomads, slept on 4000 years ago), victorious after winning his first major battle as battalion commander for Moses. It must have felt fantastic!

Have you ever had that feeling? Knowing that God used you in an epic battle? Not that you have ever been in a sword fight, but have you felt that sweet, tired, spent, intoxicating sense of accomplishment after serving our Lord? The Apostle Paul was inspired to write to his disciple Timothy that he had "fought the good fight."[122]

---

[120] Joshua 24:15.
[121] Exodus 17:8-16.
[122] 2 Timothy 4:7.

When is the last time you were in a great spiritual battle, and could say you had fought a good fight? Have you been utilizing the unique gifts our Lord has blessed you with? Those types of conflicts have significant consequences with priceless rewards. We need to hold on to what God told us through his prophet Jeremiah: *"For I know the plans I have for you, declares the LORD, plans for welfare and not for evil, to give you a future and a hope."*[123]

Because of my involvement in the world of sport, I am often asked to speak at men's events. A particular invitation came from a prominent evangelical church in Scotland to speak at a "Men's Golf Retreat." The request was to encourage the men to "grow in their faith."

The church was well known, and the chap who asked me to speak was a friend. Pulling up to the clubhouse, I realized I did not have to lock the door of my vehicle because it was obvious my car would be the last one stolen out of this parking lot.

It was a friendly affair. Nice enough guys: a little sunburned, a bit tired, polite, attentive, and best of all... they laughed at my jokes. I spoke for the expected thirty minutes, and gave them all the well-known, well-documented statistics of how the men of the church bring health to the family, community, and eternity. I employed Aristotle's "art of rhetoric": ethos, pathos, and logos. I made them laugh, made them cry, and I gave them the truth. I ended my talk with a killer-illustration, and what I thought was a sound Biblical challenge.

The golfers clapped, smiled, slapped my back, and thanked me for the "fine words." On the surface, I felt good about the night's event, but something in my gut told me I had wasted their time. The answer to what had slowly been eating at me came from a wise old man that wanted more for the men in his church than just another "'rah-rah' go-get-em-boys talk."

After all the thanks, small talk, and handshakes were over, I headed for the door, eager to get to my hotel. You know that odd feeling you get when the Holy Spirit prompts you? As I walked through the antechamber, I saw one grand old gentleman sitting in a comfortable leather chair with a sullen and somewhat cynical look on his face. Something told me to go over and say

---

[123] Jeremiah 29:11.

hello to this guy. With a big grin and my best positive-mental-attitude approach, I crossed the lobby and sat by him and asked: "How's it going, sir? You look a bit, eh—eh—well, troubled?"

This gentleman gave me the "I am not impressed look," and I thought to myself, "Boy, I wish I had never sat down with this guy!" He did not mince words but let me know that he was not thrilled with what I had to say. He went on: "Don't get me wrong, you are an okay speaker and all, but so what? This golf retreat was just another waste of time for these guys."

He informed me he was an elder at this church; had been involved with men's ministry for years; and even helped organize this golf retreat. He went on: "It was a waste of time. We have seen no fruit from these initiatives in ages."

He shifted in his chair, moved in close, and in a hushed, gruff voice, said: *We call this a retreat, but that would suggest we had been to **war**. All we do is go on **retreats**." He went on: "Steve, we don't need another **retreat**. We need to **attack**! You talked about growing spiritually, but if we don't put anything Jesus says into action, how are we to grow?"*

This wise elder was right! All I could think of was my old friend Graham, a former professional soccer player, who loves to say about Christians: "Always training—never playing."

Since the Fall of Adam and Eve, humankind has been in a war. When we duck for cover, we will never know the full extent of all we are as followers of Christ. Jesus prepared His disciples for a revolution, and they changed the world. How are we training our men and women? To duck for cover, or to serve Christ boldly?

"For we do not wrestle against flesh and blood, but against the rulers, against the authorities, against the cosmic powers over this present darkness, against the spiritual forces of evil in the heavenly places."[124]

My friend Norm loves to say: "Is your Christian life more like the 'Love Boat,' or a battleship?" I ask, does your church feel more like it is catering to the creature comforts of passengers on a cruise ship, or nurturing and training warriors in an epic battle with eternal consequences? Does the idea of fighting run counter to the Christian life? Have you seen Christians become stale for

---

[124] Ephesians 6:12.

no apparent reason? I love to ask Christians how they are to grow spiritually. The usual pat answers include things like reading the Bible, praying, and being in fellowship. Before I go any further, I believe Bible reading, prayer, and fellowship are **essential**! Unfortunately, we can engage in these disciplines and still languish!

Could it be that we are in a revolution? Could it be that the significance of fighting for God's Kingdom is far beyond what we can imagine? Could fighting for God's Kingdom be more real and more exciting, more costly, and more satisfying than any dream we can envisage? Could it be that we will never truly develop as Christians, nor understand our humanity, if we don't get into the fight?

Many church programs are passive in nature and end up dampening the grand calling our Lord has given us. The Apostle Paul kept his focus on the *rugged* message of the gospel and disciple-making. Imagine if after he got the guts kicked out of him in Lystra, he walked straight back into the city with a new strategy and said: "Forget evangelism and discipleship. The key for Asia Minor to be reached for Christ is for all the men present to meet in small clusters and take part in an accountability group to discuss our masturbation problems."

Many of our well-meaning church programs have become spiritual consumer groups with no overarching purpose. I don't think we will get any "spiritual rewards" for winning the Bible Trivia game.

There has been some healthy pushback from what has been called the "wussification of faith." Sadly, the church may be one of the first places you get castrated. How can this happen? The closer we get to God, the more revolutionary we should become. The epic themes in life—like worship, longing, love, adventure, desire, friendship, and risk—are missed when we run from a good fight. The sweetest themes in life can only be fully realized and enjoyed while grappling with a very real spiritual enemy.

Jesus says, "For whoever would save his life will lose it, but whoever loses his life for my sake will find it."[125] Our life cannot be about self-fulfillment; in fact, it is a myth that you can

---

[125] Matthew 16:25.

find self-fulfillment by seeking it. Self-fulfillment never happens in a vacuum; it is about fighting for a bigger purpose and giving yourself totally to that purpose.

FOR CONTEMPLATION:

I have watched men and women chase illusive dreams with reckless abandon down dark, dangerous roads. Perhaps worse, I have watched Christians anesthetize their souls to all that once had promise. Have you noticed that some Christians, over time, form a measure of cynicism at the gateway of their heart to guard themselves against the pain that this life can produce? If there is one dangerous place to get a callous, it is on your heart!

Others have gone looking for a fight.

- God has given you many weapons and "armor" to utilize for His kingdom purposes.
  - What is your strongest weapon?
  - Which weapons do you need to develop to become a *rugged* warrior?
- Where do you sense that God is calling you to fight? What co-*rugged* warriors can help you?
- Perhaps there is someone you have discipled that is standing on a sideline somewhere, waiting for you to contact them today?
- What are you willing to sacrifice to become a *rugged* warrior?

Chapter 14
Rugged Mind: The Great Encourager

"And the peace of God, which surpasses all understanding, will guard your hearts and your minds in Christ Jesus. Finally, brothers, whatever is true, whatever is honorable, whatever is just, whatever is pure, whatever is lovely, whatever is commendable, if there is any excellence, if there is anything worthy of praise, think about these things."[126]

I have played, coached, and have been a chaplain on almost every level of sport, and on multiple continents. On nearly every team I have been associated with, there have been a few players that love to trash-talk, players that regularly run people down verbally. A flow of negative blah-blah-blah seems to drip continuously out of their mouths, which can become toxic to those around them. Trash-talkers annoy me, primarily when they run down their own teammates. I usually approach the trash-talkers and suggest that they don't seem to have any courage. This almost always invokes a response. They often say, "What, Rev.? I have lots of courage!"

I reply, "I don't see it. If you did, you would give it away." They say, "What do you mean?" I say, "You can only give away what you possess. If you ask me for a hundred bucks, I can't give it to you—I can't give what I don't have." I usually pull out my pocket, and show them that it is empty. Then I say, "I have noticed you have never given away any courage. By the way, the root of encourage is courage. You see, I have never seen you encourage anyone. Therefore, I concluded that you don't have any courage." This usually gets them thinking. I am also quick to encourage them soon after our conversation.

I have a dear friend called Jerry, who must be the most courageous man I know; he has encouraged so many disciples.

On an early warm summer morning, I woke and couldn't wait to get out of bed. Michelle and I were hosting Jerry, his wife Claudia, and his family in our first house as newlyweds. They had

---

[126] Philippians 4:7, 8.

hosted us so many times, it was a thrill to finally return the favor. We were so honored to model the hospitality which they had frequently shown us. I wanted to make Jerry some coffee and have it ready for him when he wakened. Jerry's young family (all six of them) had arrived the previous night from Chicago. We would all be traveling to western Indiana that afternoon. I was grateful that Jerry would be the main speaker at one of my summer sports camps.

I was too late, as I vaulted down the stairs. I saw Jerry in the living room reading his Bible, coffee in hand. He looked at me as if he was in the middle of a prodigious feast. In hushed tones, since no one else was up, we spoke about what he had just read. We also discussed his prayers, and he invited me to pray with him for the young people that would attend the summer camp. His enthusiasm and appreciation for his time with God was so real and contagious, it made me want to read my Bible. The contagion has not stopped.

Jerry has written:

> *"But whether such prayers are a request for God's grace or a response to it, we cannot neglect them. God uses those prayers to bring people to Himself in a variety of ways... 'If God answered every prayer you prayed this last week, would there be anybody new in Christ's kingdom?' If we want to see people come to Christ, sacramental evangelists must be praying evangelists."[127]*

Jerry has become one of the primary authorities on C. S. Lewis; he received his doctorate writing on the problem of evil, at the Open University in Oxford, England. He is one of the first men I had met that valued the *rugged* mind.

Years earlier, while I was in college, my friend Mark had introduced me to Jerry. He was a college pastor, professor, and football coach in my hometown. I remember going into his office and being captivated. Here was a man that was wholly masculine and simultaneously academic. I was prone to dismiss academics, and loved to say, "Those that can do, those that can't teach." Jerry quickly changed my mind. His room was filled with books

---

[127] Jerry Root and Stan Guthrie, *The Sacrament of Evangelism*. Moody Publsihers, Kindle Edition, pp. 37, 38.

and reminders of his travels. He had such a generous heart: he was interested in me as a person, as an athlete, and as a Christian thinker. I always left his office with a book in my hand. Nobody had seen an intellectual side of me before. Being around, Jerry and his *rugged* intellectualism were contagious. It literally made me want to think. I asked Jerry if he would disciple me. He humbly said, "I'm not sure I can, but I am happy to be your friend." He has been discipling me ever since.

Once in his office, after a robust discussion, he said, "Steve, you have a book in you!" I said, "You mean I should read a book? Yes, you are right, Jerry, I think I should read a book." Jerry laughed and said, "No, I mean, you should write a book. You have a lot of ideas that need to be given to others." I thought he was nuts! No one had appreciated or saw potential in my mind like Jerry.[128]

He went on to say that he had a summer Bible study starting that night at his home, and would I consider team teaching it with him? That summer, I had considered going into full-time ministry, but I was not sure. I had been around a few Bible studies, and I thought, "Sure, how hard is it to teach a Bible study? This will be good for me." I agreed to team-teach.

Jerry's house was already full of college students when I arrived. They were laughing and enjoying an authentic Christian fellowship. There was an atmosphere of love and a *rugged* desire for spiritual growth in the air. Jerry and his wife Claudia have a fantastic gift for hospitality. I thought the Bible study was for a couple of college students, but there must have been forty to fifty young men and women (one-third were grad students) in his living room. I was becoming worried; I thought, "Teaching this Bible study is way over my skill level." As I wondered how I might bow out of the Bible study, Jerry announced, "This is Steve: he is my co-teacher, and by the way, I have to be gone the next four weeks." He said, "I am so grateful to the Lord that Steve has volunteered to step up and co-teach. Let's give him a big hand." I thought, "Thanks a lot, buddy—rats—no turning back now!" There were a few polite claps. Still, it was apparent that the students were disappointed that they would not be sitting under Jerry's teaching.

---

[128] To date, Steve has published eleven books.

Jerry dove into the Gospel of Matthew, and my heart sank further. He was an absolutely brilliant speaker and encourager. He had a varied mix of notable life experiences, exciting illustrations, and ironclad Biblical exegesis. I was dumbfounded, and thought, "What am I doing here?"

Jerry allowed me to use his office while he was away, I was not sure where to start with all the books on his shelf. My first attempt at the Bible study was awful; actually, I mean, I was horrible. Fortunately, most of the college students were generous and reassuring. All that summer, I would work, work out, and study the Scripture. Jerry told me, "Get the Biblical context down, and the words will follow." They didn't! At least the words didn't come at first. Slowly, I got into a groove. Now, over thirty years later, I'm still learning. When Jerry finally got back, he was very encouraging. When we disciple others, we need to let them fail without letting them feel like failures.

Traveling the world, I meet men and women that have been discipled by Jerry. He has challenged us all to be intellectually *rugged*. He is a fearless evangelist. He understands that we will have a more intimate relationship with God if we enter the spiritual battle, and desire for others to know and love Him.

> *"When we share the good news, we do not, to borrow a common expression, 'take Christ' to anyone. Remember, He is already there. The sacrament of evangelism doesn't 'do anything' to God—it does something to us. It opens our eyes to His work and grace. Those unaware of this sacrament, however, miss the opportunity to experience participating with this omnipotent, omnipresent God as He woos others to Himself. It is not a question of whether God is at work in His world. It is a question of whether those who claim to follow Him will participate with Him in this sacrament."*[129]

Not only is Jerry a *rugged* academic; he is active in loads of other pursuits. His interests in music, art, architecture, sports, and theater are contagious. I don't remember him demanding that I should read a particular book or watch a specific movie.

---

[129] Jerry Root and Stan Guthrie, Ibid., p. 17.

He is so enthusiastic that his interests are infectious, and spill over into your world, making your life more profound. He is selective, but he loves movies with redemptive themes, and how they seem to resonate within society. He wants to learn about most things which broaden his mind, and this gives him a bridge to relationships with a wide variety of people. I have seen him build friendships with garbagemen and opera singers. His unvarnished passion for Jesus, Scripture, and culture encouraged me to study harder and appreciate things beyond my scope.

Transparency has always been important to Jerry; he dislikes pretense. This is a rare quality among professors and pastors. I have seen him frustrated and wrestling with sin in his own life, which makes him all the more human. "I can relate to an imperfect person because I am imperfect," he will often tell me. Watching Jerry wrestle with sin makes me want to fight with my own sin and live more like Jesus. Jerry's openness has made me more courageous to be more transparent with the guys I disciple.

> *Jerry's openness has made me more courageous to be more transparent with the guys I disciple.*

Not only has Jerry encouraged me academically, he would also visit me when I was with the Chicago Bears. He was there when I chose a wife. He gave us family guidance, and he has held each of my children as babies; they still call him Uncle Jerry. When I was honored with my doctorate, he was there. Jerry has been present when I have spoken at high-profile events, including preaching to the future king of England. Wherever Jerry has watched me speak, there has been an enormous smile of encouragement on his face. At each event that he has encouraged me, I couldn't help but think he should be the one speaking. Perhaps he is.

POSTSCRIPT:

My dog has a mind; his name is Opie. Whenever I grab the food scoop, my bulldog's stubby little tail starts to wag. Though my dog can think, I doubt I will ever receive a poem in his bowl reflecting his gastronomic appreciation. Humans, as a species, also have a mind, *"God created man in his own image,"*[130] and are, therefore, rational beings. A central aspect of human rationality is the ability to apprehend and reflect great abstract ideas. When it comes to thinking, the Bible tells us there is a bifurcation (a fork in the road): one by the unregenerate mind, and one by the regenerate mind.

Remember that "sin breaks everything," including our thinking. Sin has a drastic effect on our cognitive ability to think objectively, as Paul was inspired to write: *"They became futile in their thinking, and their foolish hearts were darkened."*[131] Consequently, the unregenerate human has a limited cognitive foundation, as Paul further elaborates in his letter to the Romans: *"They exchanged the truth about God for a lie and worshiped and served created things rather than the Creator..."*[132] Moses states that the life of those far from God is a world of self-deception and deliberate suppression of the truth, and it results in an understanding that is darkened: *"For the intention of man's heart is evil from his youth."*[133] Paul was inspired to write to the Ephesians to instruct them that the unregenerate mind is "futile." *"Now this I say and testify in the Lord, that you must no longer walk as the Gentiles do, in the futility of their minds."*[134]

As regenerate persons, we must never have an arrogant, self-righteous attitude. We must feel blessed and understand any spiritual insight we may possess is *"all from God."*[135] Illumination is a beautiful gift given to us by the Holy Spirit. Therefore, we must have the attitude of Peter which he writes about in his first epistle: *"Always being prepared to make a defense to anyone who asks ... yet do it with gentleness and respect."*[136] The old expression Jerry often said to me was: "We are merely one beggar showing another beggar where the bread is."

Nevertheless, Luke points out that the Christian intellect is unique, and has supernatural insight: *"And their eyes were*

---

[130] Genesis 1:27.
[131] Romans 1:21.
[132] Romans 1:25.
[133] Genesis 8:21.
[134] Ephesians 4:17.
[135] John 3:16; Ephesians 2:4.
[136] 1 Peter 3:15.

opened, and they recognized him. "[137] No one emphasizes that
more than the Apostle Paul as he expressed it in his letter to the
Romans. Paul transitions his letter from explaining God's grace,[138]
to encouraging his readers on how we as Christians should live in
response to grace (unmerited favor). He was inspired to write that
we are to: *"present your bodies as a living sacrifice..."*[139]

Paul draws our attention back to the past eleven
chapters, where he philosophically as well as spiritually unpacks
grace, mankind's desperate need for salvation, and our inability
to save ourselves. It is, indeed, God's *"free gift."*[140]

The Jewish recipients of Paul's letter to the Romans
would have immediately understood the "sacrificial system."
Yet they would have been shocked to read that they were to be a
"living sacrifice." We are to give all of our being, not just an
annual sacrifice, to God. The sacrifice of our whole self is not
performance-based, but rather, a response of gratitude to God's
endless mercy.

Our lives can be compartmentalized; we often
underappreciate the mind. Some would say that Christians are
actually a bunch of anti-intellectuals. Jesus gives us the ultimate
big picture when a scribe asked Him, "What is the greatest
commandment?" In an economy of words, Jesus quotes
Deuteronomy 6:5: *"'You shall love the Lord your God with all
your heart and with all your soul and with all your mind... And
a second is like it: You shall love your neighbor as yourself.'"*[141]
We are to love God with all our being, heart, soul, mind,
strength, and neighbor.

The Apostle Paul continues to explain the importance of
the mind for worshiping God. You can only be "transformed"
into the *"image of God"*[142] *"by the renewal of your mind."*[143]

The word "transformed" is like a caterpillar
metamorphosing into a butterfly. I often ask my disciples, "Do

---

[137] Luke 24:31.
[138] Romans 12:1, 2.
[139] Ibid.
[140] Romans 6:23.
[141] Matthew 22:37-39.
[142] Genesis 1:26-28.
[143] Romans 12:2.

you want to be a worm, or a butterfly? Do you want to crawl, or fly?"

We are renewable creatures. The human machine continues to need oxygen, water, food—if you do not believe me, just stop breathing for eight minutes.

How do we renew our minds? Paul first suggests we take off the "old self." Here he is talking about repentance.[144] Yet, we do not stop there; we must put on the "new self" by *keeping our attention and focus on Jesus Christ.* All things were made by Him and for Him. Jesus is our Righteousness, our Foundation, and we center our minds on Him. Jesus is Lord and sits at the right hand of the Father.[145] We think and meditate on such things, we sing of such things, we proclaim such things, and our lives are predicated on such matters.

We open our hearts/minds to the living God. Aren't you glad God gave us a book! But not so fast—there is more! Christians have a Bible that is illuminated by the Holy Spirit. One of the ministries of the Holy Spirit is opening our minds to the *"living and active"* Word of God.[146] The Holy Spirit, like a flashlight, is pointing to the Bible in a dark room, illuminating the Scripture to help us understand and live out the blueprint for the human machine.

> Aren't you glad God gave us a book!

After I became a Christian, I was amazed at how the Bible came alive. A friend of mine, Brad, was a longtime NFL football player for the Cincinnati Bengals. His position coach, a Christian, would pick and write a new Scripture on his whiteboard every season. Season after season, hour after hour Brad would sit in meetings and sometimes glance at the Scripture, speculating on what it meant in the context of his life. Eventually, Brad became a Christian through their chapel program. All of a sudden, those Scriptures, which had once befuddled him, started flooding back into his mind with clarity, purpose, and comfort.

To transform, we need to allow God to restore us spiritually. The gateway to restoration is the mind. Paul goes on to say that an incredible byproduct of spiritual renewal is "discernment." The more we are renewed and have the *"mind of*

---

[144] Ephesians 4:22-24.
[145] Romans 8:34.
[146] Hebrews 4:12.

Christ, "[147] the more we understand what is best for our well-being (*"good, acceptable, perfect"*) and the welfare of our world.

Proverbs 4:23 reminds us to: *"Keep [guard] your heart with all vigilance..."* The heart is understood to be the mind. What does it mean to guard our mind? Imagine that you were the bodyguard for a baby princess. Your job was to guard the baby against evil forces that wanted to destroy her. Your duty would be to stay diligent, be discerning and protective. The honorable person would do his very best to guard and care for the baby princess, perhaps even giving his very life for the protection of the infant.

In the same way, we are instructed to guard our minds. Are we as diligent, discerning, and attentive, protecting our minds as we would a little baby? Do we actually value our mind enough to guard it?

What are we allowing to enter into our minds that imperceptibly nudges us away from God? If you were physically sitting down with Jesus, which media programming would you enjoy together? Which media would you be ashamed of if Jesus were physically in the room? Which relationships are subtly pushing you away from your devotion to God? Which relationships encourage your relationship with Jesus?

With extreme prejudice, Satan wants to destroy Christians. Peter knows something about being "sifted" by Satan and turning his back on Jesus. He humbly warns us: *"Be sober-minded; be watchful. Your adversary, the devil, prowls around like a roaring lion, seeking someone to devour."*[148]

We are not to merely prohibit negative influences on the mind; we are to cultivate and fill the mind with good eternal virtues as Paul writes to the believers in Philippi: *"Brothers, whatever is true, whatever is honorable, whatever is just, whatever is pure, whatever is lovely, whatever is commendable, if there is any excellence, if there is anything worthy of praise, think about these things."*[149]

The mind is a fantastic instrument. We are learning that there are pitfalls by coaching with a negative attitude. I know

---

[147] Philippians 2:5-8.
[148] 1 Peter 5:8.
[149] Philippians 4:8.

several coaches who are becoming aware of the power of positive coaching. Coaches want to succeed, and many are training themselves and their staff to teach with a more strategically positive attitude. For example, if we say to a running back on an American football team that he shouldn't run like a weakling, and he should never fumble the ball, we have just put two negative images in his mind: "weak" and "fumble." We know it is much more useful to teach the positive, "Run *hard*, and carry the ball *tight*." I have seen coaches work hard at creating and teaching positive, *rugged* imagery.

Why should this surprise us? Scripture has been warning us about negative input from the beginning. Are you filling your mind with *rugged*, positive, godly imagery? How are you encouraging those you disciple to protect and renew their minds?

A *rugged* mind means to cultivate the mind with anything that brings us closer to God. *Rugged* intellectualism does not mean "intellectual elitism." Our attitude is always as a humble servant. Nor does *rugged* thinking mean we should be isolationists. The place God puts us, especially some locker rooms, can be a harsh spiritual environment. We are to be active in spreading God's Word wherever God strategically places us. All the more, we need to cultivate the mind to be prepared for battle.

This is not the dangerous pseudo-religion of positive mental attitude. I am not saying, "Think happy thoughts, and they shall appear." Instead, we are allowing our Lord to saturate our life with prayer, Biblical study, and beautiful images, music, and stories that help to renew our mind. To be a disciple and disciple-maker is to encourage these spiritual disciplines.

Reading the Bible is renewing, but when we do it with someone who will, in turn, live out what he has learned, it is transformational and inspiring. For example, throughout much of Jesus' ministry, the crowds continually pressed upon Him. At times He was exhausted. On Jesus' final trip to Jerusalem, another large and needy group had gathered, the disciples were tired, and presumably, Jesus was also tired. When mothers heard that Jesus was in their vicinity, they streamed to Jesus to get their little children blessed. The weary and exacerbated disciples had had enough and turned the mothers away. Jesus famously rebuked them and encouraged the children to come to Him, sit with Him, and receive a blessing.[150] This example of patience and compassion must have been an excellent lesson for the disciples, who later would find themselves caring for multitudes of needy people in arduous and dangerous circumstances. Their minds had experienced a living sermon.

I have read hundreds of times the upper-room narrative, and imagined Jesus washing the disciples' feet. In my mind's eye, I have heard Jesus say several times: *"For I have given you an example, that you also should do just as I have done to you."*[151]

Jerry models servanthood. I have watched Jerry, after speaking at events, take time with everyone that wanted to talk to him, and there is usually a long line. He is always gracious and makes himself available. This has helped me to better serve my students after a lecture or after a speaking event. I have read, *"Husbands, love your wives, as Christ loved the church and gave himself up for her..."*[152] It has been inspiring watching Jerry treat his family and wife Claudia with love and respect. There are times I don't feel like loving Michelle, but I draw on Scripture and Jerry's example. Again, the Apostle Paul said: *"Be imitators of me, as I am of Christ."*[153]

FOR CONTEMPLATION:

Allowing the Holy Spirit to open your mind to Scripture, and to experience examples of *rugged*, mature Christians living out the Word, is powerful and transformative. Letting the very essence of another human's devotion to God, powered by the Word of God, pour into your heart and mind, is at the heart of Jesus' model of disciple-making.

- How can you pour courage into the person you are discipling today?
- Have you listened well to those you are discipling?
  - Have you encouraged their ideas, dreams, and thoughts?
- Are you trying to impress those you are discipling with your intellect or are you genuinely encouraging those discipling to cultivate their minds for Christ?

---

[150] Matthew 19:14.
[151] John 13:15.
[152] Ephesians 5:25.
[153] 1 Corinthians 11:1.

Chapter 15
Rugged Pioneers: Learning to Disciple Others, Though You May Have Never Been Discipled Yourself

"When he saw the crowds, he had compassion for them, because they were harassed and helpless, like sheep without a shepherd. Then he said to his disciples, 'The harvest is plentiful, but the laborers are few; therefore pray earnestly to the Lord of the harvest to send out laborers into his harvest.'"[154]

"Necessity is the mother of invention."[155]

No Role Model

My friend David is the best youth baseball coach I have ever seen. He is technically brilliant and has a sincere love for his young athletes. Over the years, I have watched him take groups of under-skilled children, and transform them into happy and talented teams. He sees his young players as not just a group of athletes that have the potential to win league championships, but more so, he sees them as disciples, future fathers, future mothers, and even future servants for the Kingdom of God.

At lunch one day, I asked him about his experience as a baseball player. I was surprised to hear that he never played organized baseball. "So how did you become such a great coach, having never played?" David just grinned and said: "I just love the game!"

David's father was never involved in athletics, and he was never encouraged to play. David's family was not well off. He had to work as a kid and did not have time for much else. He had to learn to coach on his own.

I next asked him if he'd had a spiritual disciple/mentor in his life growing up. David told me that, regretfully, he didn't really have anybody intentionally walk with him as a young Christian. "I stumbled into a church youth group, heard the

---

[154] Matthew 9:36-38
[155] Old British proverb.

gospel, and asked Christ into my life," he said. David went on to say: "Before I knew it, I was their youth pastor. Sadly, that church fell apart, and I just had to figure out how to encourage other Christians on my own." David had a passion for God, for kids, and for baseball, so he learned to become a great coach and disciple-maker even though he had never been coached or discipled himself.

Jesus trained His disciples to, *"Therefore pray earnestly to the Lord of the harvest to send out laborers into his harvest."*[156] As we have seen, there is a recurring dilemma throughout the history of the church. There are more harvest fields than workers.

Sadly, many Christians never experience Christ's model of discipleship. Unfortunately, the bridge to spiritual maturity is an all too lonely road for the majority of Christ-followers. Far too many Christ-followers have not had the privilege of a mature Christian to encourage and guide them towards spiritual maturity. Because of this problem, many young Christians never seem to mature in their faith.

Understand that the lack of disciple-makers is not a new or purely American dilemma; it has been a global dilemma since the beginning of the Christian church. There are so few Christians that understand or are willing to help young converts cross the bridge into spiritual maturity, and become *"rooted and built up..."*[157]

Aren't you glad Jesus had discipled those twelve men (and countless other men and women)! You may have never had someone to disciple you, but that does not disqualify you from making disciples. In fact, if only those that have had disciple relationships were allowed to make disciples, large segments of the world would never be discipled!

Cambodian Pioneers

Sport is everywhere on the planet, so sports ministry has taken me all over the world. When I was invited by friends to do leadership training in Cambodia, I was thrilled. It is always an honor to engage with young leaders and help them develop their ministries. However, on this particular trip, while observing the

---

[156] Matthew 9:38.
[157] Colossians 2:7.

rugged Cambodian students live out their faith, I became very angry.

Cambodian Christians have very few models to emulate. This is understandable since former Cambodian leader Pol Pot almost destroyed his country. His radical, communist government, the Khmer Rouge, had displaced millions through forced evacuations of major cities to "cleanse" the Khmer people from external influences. Even more horribly, over 1.5 million people were executed, and countless more starved to death in his brutal regime. From 1975 to 1979, Pol Pot systematically killed the majority of every college educated person. Thousands of teachers, and more than 90 percent of the small but bold Christian population, disappeared. Pol Pot almost succeeded in "cleansing" the entire Christian community from his country. Author and missionary Don Cormack, in his eyewitness account documented in *Killing Fields, Living Fields*, estimated that only a few indigenous Christian leaders survived the brutal carnage.[158]

Watching Cambodia's resilient people climb out of horrific adversity is inspiring and humbling. The Christians of Cambodia are indeed *rugged*, and their numbers are growing again. So, you can understand one of the causes of my anger, but also my excitement. During my first trip to Cambodia, I was perplexed, encouraged, and challenged to see the vitality of a new wave of young Christian leaders emerge.

Because the Cambodian church currently is in need of more workers, it is inevitable that some people will need to learn how to make disciples, though they have never been discipled themselves. Training is crucial. In Cambodia, I saw many leaders that had the same experience as my friend David, the baseball coach. They were learning to disciple others, though they had never experienced a genuine discipleship relationship themselves. They had to grow on their own, but they were eager to learn.

As I climbed onto our bus heading south, I was met with the smell of stale fish, dust, and diesel fumes. I was joining several Cambodian college students in a jam-packed journey to the hostel we had rented for our training week. We were traveling from the capital, Phnom Penh, to Cambodia's southern

---

[158] Don Cormack, *Killing Fields, Living Fields: Faith in Cambodia.*

coast. With the help of a talented interpreter, we quickly got to know each other, and the journey flew by quickly.

We enjoyed each other's company, and most of the Cambodians were warmly inquisitive and possessed a friendly dignity, which seemed especially familiar to their region. They certainly weren't complaining about the heat, crowded environment, or smelly fish. The students were curious about my life in the West, and they kept asking me about my own disciple experience.

These young college leaders naturally assumed that because I was a westerner, I had been discipled: as if it were a prerequisite that all Christians outside of Cambodia had enjoyed a wonderful discipleship experience. They were shocked to hear that every Christian outside of Cambodia had not received a disciple relationship. I was ashamed as I tried to explain why not all western Christians had been discipled.

Two of the students in particular, Amos and Vithu, wanted to know how I became a Christian, and how I had matured. They asked who had discipled me, and for how long; what was the process like; did I live with my teacher; and was the process the same in America and Europe?

Since disciple-making has always been near and dear to my heart, this was a refreshing and rare series of conversations. Most people I meet abroad want to know about Chicago, Hollywood, basketball stars, and how many of those stars I knew personally. "Do you know LeBron?"

I asked Amos and Vithu: "I see disciple-making is very important to you. So, who discipled you, and whom are you discipling?" They answered in a matter-of-fact way that neither of them had been discipled. "No, we are just now learning about discipleship," they said. "Some of us have pastors, but they are so busy. They tell us 'go and learn how to disciple yourselves, and then go disciple others.' So we are learning."

I thought about the amazing men and women that had encouraged me, and still do. I thought about the devotion these young Cambodian students had to our Creator, and how they were taking the Great Commission so seriously. It was refreshing to hear how these students were learning to disciple others, though they had never been discipled themselves.

The conference was lively. The students were serious about learning and putting into practice what they heard. We examined the amazing life of Christ with His disciples. We examined the spiritual ingredients that Jesus employed, and tried to figure out how we could put these concepts into action in 21st-century Cambodia. Some of my stories were lost in translation, but we stayed close to Biblical principles, which are timeless and universal. It indeed was a rich and moving experience for me.

One night on a break from the conference, I found myself bobbing up and down gently in the waters of the Gulf of Thailand, watching a beautiful sunset, and discussing the Great Commission with Amos and Vithu. The beach was horribly littered, but the water was lovely, and the training was going well. I was feeling relaxed and enjoying hanging out with my new friends. We appreciated the break after many hours of lectures, good discussion, and experiential learning. Their love for God was unmistakable, and their response to that love was a manifest desire to help others love Jesus. Both of these men had become Christians at their college, and both had a passion for reaching and redeeming their country for Christ.

As I was floating in the ocean, I said to Vithu: "Hey, this is beautiful; do you come to this beach often?"

Vithu replied: "It is beautiful! But this is the first time I have ever experienced it."

I asked: "You mean this beach?"

He answered: "No, it is the first time I ever seen the sea. I live in Phnom Pen, and this is the furthest I have ever traveled in my life."

I came from a working-class family in Chicago and had not traveled much either as a youth. I also remember the first time I saw the ocean. I was 17 years old and was flying into Los Angeles International Airport for a college football game with seventy-five other teammates. I think the whole team had their faces pressed into the window, looking out at the Pacific Ocean. The Pacific was fantastic, but I think we were more interested in trying to find those beautiful southern California girls that we had heard about all our lives.

Amos chimed in: "Yes, me, too. This is my first time in the ocean. It is a good experience. It's wonderful!"

I asked my two rookie beach bums: "Hey, you think there are sharks here in the Gulf of Thailand?"

Amos, whose English was a bit clearer, said: "Haaaa, sarks (sharks). I asked my cousin who travels a lot if there were sarks in this sea, and she says they only bite at sunset."

I replied: "Isn't this sunset?"

They looked at each other, gave me an anxious nod, and then raced to the shore as fast as they could. I'm pretty sure I beat them back to the beach!

Safely back on shore, the three of us continued to talk about their plans for developing small faith communities around Cambodia. They focused on meeting people in cities and villages, building relationships, and sharing the gospel message, but they were not finished. Their plan was not to fill up a church with followers; they also wanted workers who could participate in the maturation of the young Christians. They understood that the key was building a *rugged* community of Christians who could "produce reproducing reproducers."[159]

This was not mere theory for my young Cambodian students. They were doing it. They both played soccer, and through the relationships which were quickly built through competition, they were creating a strong bond with their teammates. Over time they were starting to share Christ and build up a small fellowship of believers.

I am not sure if my training was memorable, but their obedience was unforgettable, and the young pioneers left an indelible mark of encouragement on me. It wasn't until I got on the plane and headed back to the West that I started to get angry. I was struck by a sad realization: for much of my adult life, I have been teaching at Christian events all over the world. I noticed one disturbing similarity between the young Cambodian Christian leaders and the young Christian leaders in the West: They were both trying to answer God's Great Commission of making disciples, though most of them had never been discipled themselves.

Like their Cambodian peers, many young Western Christian leaders are committed to obeying Christ and are passionate about the Great Commission. They also have never

---

[159] This is one of CSRM's greatest mantras!

been discipled, and like their Cambodian counterparts, are learning to disciple though nobody has discipled them. It certainly is understandable that the Cambodians have so few models of discipleship due to their country's history of genocide, but what excuse do we have in the West?

> *It certainly is understandable that the Cambodians have so few models of discipleship due to their country's history of genocide, but what excuse do we have in the West?*

The Cambodian people carry physical and mental scars from the reign of Pol Pot to this day, and few Christians survived. It is understandable that young Cambodian Christians have to disciple others though they have never been discipled themselves, but the question must be asked: where were the Christian leaders in the West? Cambodian Christians were slaughtered, while we were living a life of wealth and self-gratification. Why have so many people in the West not had a discipleship experience?

It is understandable when only a handful of Christian leaders survive a holocaust, that the young Christians in Cambodia will have to find their way without a shepherd. However, it seems criminal that Western youth, with such a high proportion of Christians, have had to do the same thing. They have to disciple others though they have never been discipled themselves.

My guess is, if you are reading a book about discipleship, you are currently involved in, or at least interested in, the Great Commission. Maybe you have had mentors in your life, and the rich experience of a guide, teacher, encourager, so making disciples comes naturally to you. Or sadly, like so many, you may have never had a healthy discipleship experience. Somehow, by God's grace, you landed in "the good soil," and your faith has taken root. Of course, you, too, like my Cambodian friends, can learn and participate in God's grand strategy "to go and make disciples." To my generation's shame, you will have to learn without the luxury of experience. Nonetheless, a new wave of ministry innovators is emerging. We need you to break the cycle of lethargy and be a disciple-making pioneer in the lives of those around you. By the power of the Holy Spirit, you can encourage young people to worship and serve our King. Be part of that emerging generation that gives themselves totally to serving God and helping others to love Him with all their hearts.

Jesus said, *"the laborers are few."*[160] Some jobs become unnecessary over time, but making disciples and pleading with God to give us more workers in His harvest fields are things that will always be desperately needed. Like many parts of the world, the Cambodians are struggling to find role models. They understand their challenges, and they are not making excuses. They are breaking the cycle of spiritual inactivity and moving towards a model that the rest of the world may someday follow. They are answering God's call and walking in the steps of great Christian men and women who came before them, and somehow, some way, they are making *rugged* disciples.

Can you become a great disciple-maker even though you may have never been discipled? Remember, when I asked my friend David how he became a great coach though he had never played baseball as a youth? He said, "I just loved the game." How do we become great disciple-makers? Loving God and loving others is the best start.

POSTSCRIPT:

"'Come, I will send you to Pharaoh that you may bring my people, the children of Israel, out of Egypt.' But Moses said to God, 'Who am I that I should go to Pharaoh and bring the children of Israel out of Egypt?'"[161]

My coach told me excuses were like elbows: we all had two of them. It seems Moses had more excuses than elbows. The most famous character in the Old Testament felt utterly unqualified for the task God had given him and would undoubtedly be happy to sit on the sidelines and let someone else do God's bidding. Moses was throwing out a ton of excuses for why he was not the man for the job. It took some encouraging by God, but Moses managed to free the Israelites and, over time and through adversity; God shaped a powerful and culturally magnificent nation. Moses became a Biblical hero, but poor

---

[160] Matthew 9:37.
[161] Exodus 3:10, 11.

Moses had no human role model to help guide him towards this colossal task. These were uncharted waters he had to navigate.

> *Moses became a Biblical hero, but poor Moses had no human role model to guide him towards this colossal task.*

For the past forty years he had been watching sheep in the wilderness, literally. Now God wanted him to go up against the arguably the greatest force in the known world, Pharaoh and his kingdom, and free and lead his people to the Promised Land. Who wouldn't feel inadequate?

God didn't tell Moses that Moses would rescue the Jews. God said, *"And I have come down to deliver them out of the hand of the Egyptians..."*[162] His tool/pawn for rescue was Moses. He chose Moses to be their leader, though Moses felt totally unqualified. We, too, can have the privilege to be a pioneer for God, though we may also feel inadequate.

God most certainly is asking you to participate in His magnificent mission. You, like Moses, may feel unqualified for the job. You also may feel you are in uncharted water—that is not a bad sign. It means you understand that you are a mere pawn in the hand of the Master. Didn't you wake up this morning saying you wanted to be a pawn?

You may think being a pawn is a pejorative term for a "nobody," but it originates from the Latin word "foot soldier;" someone who was first into battle (we also get "peon" from the same word). The word eventually morphed into the most awesome of words: "pioneer."

FOR CONTEMPLATION:

As a young Christian, I also wrongly assumed that every Christian had someone to help him in his Christian faith. Now

> *Are you willing to be a pioneer?*

I understand it is a rare privilege. You may have never had the opportunity of an authentic discipleship experience, but that doesn't mean you can't disciple others or find someone to disciple you! You will have to be a pawn/pioneer! Pioneers go to places where no one else has gone.

---

[162] Exodus 3:8.

God's pawns/pioneers always understand that though they may feel inadequate, they have the hand of God masterfully controlling their next move.

- Do you feel disqualified to make disciples because you
- were never discipled?
- Which young potential leaders can you encourage today?
- Whom can you meet with (this month) who will encourage you? Make that phone call.

Chapter 16
Rugged Grace: Dead Dogs and Stolen Motorcycles

"But God, being rich in mercy, because of the great love with which he loved us, even when we were dead in our trespasses, made us alive together with Christ—by grace you have been saved—and raised us up with him and seated us with him in the heavenly places in Christ Jesus."[163]

The best way to understand a principle is indeed to experience it. The concept of grace usually runs counterintuitive to our experience. Sadly, many have never encountered it; all they know is the law and self-sufficiency. Sometimes it's the small examples of grace that help us remember His amazing grace. Once upon a time, I experienced grace in the rough-and-tumble city of Sophia, Bulgaria.

They never taught me about this in seminary when I was studying to be a pastor! It was a Saturday night, and my friends were waiting for my arrival. I was on my motorcycle, part of a four-thousand-mile

> *They never taught me about this in seminary!*

round trip between Scotland and Turkey, to visit friends, and lecture at a couple of Bible schools. I had just purchased a brand-new BMW motorcycle, and I couldn't wait to get on the road. The trip was uneventful until I reached Bulgaria; then it was full of grace!

I was stuck at the Romanian/Bulgarian border Saturday night with long lines of migrants trying to cross. The trip was challenging. I could not find any accommodation, so I unrolled my sleeping bag and slept in a watermelon field near a Romanian border town. Little did I know that the border delay was only the beginning of an incredible week-long adventure.

Instead of leaving Tuesday as planned, I was stuck in Sofia until Friday at 2 p.m. My friends Bob and Becky and their young family were missionaries in Bulgaria, and had only lived in

---

[163] Ephesians 2:4-6.

Sophia, the capital city of well over a million people, for about two months. They were looking forward to seeing a familiar face.

Eastern Europe is ever changing; as I traveled on my motorcycle, half the vehicles I passed would have been horse and cart. Entering Sophia, the contrast between "old world" farmers and gypsies slowly transitioned to "new world," high-rises, affluence, drugs, and prostitutes.

Now in Sofia, I was lost in a maze of buildings; the Bulgarian alphabet is Cyrillic, not Roman, so Bob and Becky told me to find a "landmark," and they would find me. Eventually, I saw a familiar sign: the ubiquitous McDonald's restaurant you see in the city center of almost every European capital city. As I tried to park, I was cut off by a man driving a Porsche and wearing an Armani suit. I don't really know if it was Armani; it was just way more beautiful than any suit that I have ever owned. The man jumped out of the car with a bit of swagger, yelled at me with an Eastern European accent, and said: "Man, you gotta be quick in Sophia." He then sauntered into the McDonald's. I managed to park nearby, and tried to call Bob, eventually getting a clear phone connection. While I waited for my buddy to lead me to their apartment, I actually managed to have a friendly, if brief, conversation with the man in the Armani suit about Christ.

Another hour later, Bob and I reunited like long lost friends. Bob told me to "follow him." I was impressed at how quickly he had adapted to the aggressive style of driving, as we zoomed through the city traffic, late Sunday night. Once at Bob and Becky's flat, we secured the motorcycle with his giant lock and cable in their steel door garage. Bob then pulled his car up to the door, and we went upstairs, talked for hours, and finally went to sleep.

Monday morning, Becky woke Bob with a question: "Where did Steve go on his bike this morning?" He answered: "Nowhere," since he was sure I was still asleep in the guest room. Then she said: "But the garage is open, and it's empty!" At that he jumped out of bed, dreading that the motorcycle had been stolen. Unfortunately, it was. I was probably tailed from the border of Romania or the center of Sophia (Armani man); the thieves were real pros and followed us to their apartment in

141

their gated compound. They waited until it was really late, and broke in.

With an acetylene torch, they burned a hole through the first garage door (a neighbor and a Member of Parliament for Bulgaria, with a nice car), looked inside, and went to the next garage door, Bob's. They burned a hole in his garage door, saw the brand-new BMW motorcycle, and broke it open. The thieves then shoved Bob's van out of the way, opened the garage door, sprayed liquid nitrogen on the lock, and after freezing it, tapped it with a hammer, and it quickly shattered. Next, they ripped out the ignition, and stole the motorcycle! Gone in 60 seconds!

That was a dreadful morning, I still remember Bob, who is customarily a cool and cheerful man, frantically waking me with the bad news. There was a wrenching in my gut as I felt like I was sinking in quicksand, and it got worse. When I called home, I found out there were two countries my insurance was invalid: Romania and Bulgaria!

I also bought insurance at the border, just to be on the safe side. Unfortunately, when we went to the police, they just laughed. They told us the insurance wasn't worth the paper it was printed on, and quietly advised us to go to the Mafia or buy a ticket home.

So that is what we did: we contacted the Mafia. A friend, Tony, who was a new Christian, and worked at Bob's seminary, had formerly worked in the "auto business" in the murky underworld of the Mafia. So, with a little persuasion, the Sophia mob put out a manhunt for the thieves, and we had a nervous 24 hours of waiting. We kept calling, but the Mafia assured us they would find the bike; that the thieves were now sleeping; that they have been "working" all night, and we shouldn't worry! A day and a night later, both the thieves and the bike were located. Getting it back was another trial.

The thieves were probably surprised, and more than a little bit nervous that the Mafia was on to them so quickly in search of a foreign bike. Vehicles from outside the country are considered "fair game" for thieves in Sophia, and foreigners typically have no recourse other than to file a theft report with the local police. Such cases are rarely solved.

After the bike was identified, we had a protracted negotiation to determine the price (read ransom) for the return of the motorcycle, which continued until Wednesday morning.

The big problem was that I simply did not have the money and could not afford the ransom. I was ashamed to not have purchased the right insurance, and embarrassed that I had brought such turmoil to such a beautiful missionary family so soon after they arrived in Sophia. I could not let them pay the ransom, but I knew I would lose the bike and have three years of payments for nothing. Bob insisted he had the funds, and he wanted to pay the ransom. It was hard on my pride, but I eventually relented. I wondered why Bob would want to help a dead dog like me! Bob went to the bank.

After agreeing to terms, we scheduled the ransom drop, and returned for late Wednesday night. At just a little before 11 p.m., our friend Tony met us at Bob and Becky's flat, and for the next three hours, we engaged in an anxious game of cat and mouse.

Communication was only through an intermediary, a friend of Tony's with links to the Mafia. This link, "Ivan," received instructions via mobile phone, and passed them on to us. At no time were we ever in direct contact with either the Mafia or the thieves.

First, we waited near Bob's home on Milin Kamuk Street, the three of us in Tony's small Fiat, and Ivan with a passenger (bodyguard) in another little beat-up Citron. Then we had to pass the money to the thieves through Ivan, so it could be counted and inspected for "marks."

None of us liked the idea of giving up the money before getting our hands on the bike, but we didn't seem to have any choice. We were convinced the thieves would take the money and keep the bike too, but Ivan reassured us, by pointing out that the thieves had struck the deal through the Mafia, and if they reneged there would be dangerous ramifications for them. Ivan told us that if they played games, he knew some people who played such games, and we'd have both the money and the bike back by tomorrow. Faced with such simple logic, we agreed to let Ivan take them the money. Even so, Ivan called to tease us about our being a bit nervous now! Ha, ha! We were.

Soon we were led zooming around the city to see if police were tailing us. Next, we were told the bike was "somewhere uptown," so off we went. Then having passed the test, and the thieves were sure we were not tailed, we were directed to the McDonalds.

All of a sudden there seemed to be police everywhere, and the thieves called Ivan, who called us, worried, to make sure there wasn't any double-cross afoot. At one point while driving around, we were stopped, and Ivan, who was driving an unregistered car, had to bribe the police to keep them from impounding his vehicle! After waiting for what seemed to be a long time, the thieves called to say there were still too many police around, and we should return to the place from which the bike was stolen. Off we drove again to Milin Kamuk. Once there, they called to say the bike was outside somewhere around our block, so we circled the neighborhood for a few minutes, peering into the shadows, trying to spy the motorcycle.

Then they called with additional instructions for us to get back to McDonald's as fast as we could! We thought the thieves picked up my trail when I stopped at the McDonald's downtown on arrival, so the use of a McDonald's for the return injected a kind of poetry into the whole situation.

So, we raced over, and as we pulled in, we saw a solitary bike parked two-thirds of the way down the lot, as if the owner had just stepped inside for a quick bite. We could hardly believe it. Was it okay? Was it really there? We kept our emotions in check until we got right up to it to see that indeed it was my motorcycle, and it looked to be without a scratch on it.

There were high fives and backslaps all around as happiness and relief overwhelmed us, and the reality of having recovered the bike began to sink in. It was 3:30 a.m. The first thing I did was wake up my wife Michelle back in Scotland and tell her the good news. She cried.

It took some work to get the bike started since the thieves had stripped the ignition to steal it; then we returned it to the garage, now fitted with a new steel door, for the night. Bob and I set out mattresses and sleeping bags in the garage, not willing to leave the bike alone again. We sat up almost until dawn before being able to sleep.

Crime makes for strange bedfellows, and later we began to dwell on the ethics of what we did. We contracted with a criminal organization to apprehend thieves outside the system of law. Was it right? Was it good? Would we do it again? Maybe time will reveal insights we aren't yet able to recognize, but for now, we wait, unable to know for sure. One thing, though: I'll always remember the happiness of our small band of conspirators as we surrounded that bike in the parking lot. What a tremendous sense of satisfaction! We had taken a risk, and everything fell into place. The bike was back. Of course, compared to heaven, this story is of small consequence, but whenever I hear of grace, I think about Bob's grace to me and our adventure. Even now, it makes me smile.

POSTSCRIPT:

What does the above story teach me about grace? I was stupid enough to arrive on a new motorcycle in Bulgaria without completely understanding the insurance and putting both Bob and his family at risk. Bob paid the "ransom" for my bike, and never mentioned it again.

It is easier to teach a child the idea of friendship to one who has experienced a kind friend. It is easier to teach the principle of love to a child that has been loved. The concept of gravity is more easily understood after one has taken a tumble. In this world of no pain, no gain; hard work equals reward; smart kids get A's; dumb kids get D's; attractive men get attractive women—we have a hard time experiencing and understanding grace. In the "meritorious" world we live in, "grace" is a principle that is rarely recognized or valued. The technical term for grace is "unmerited favor," getting something you do not deserve—the principle is almost totally unique to Christianity.

The young orphan bows before the high king, and says, *"What is your servant, that you should show regard for a dead dog such as I?"*[164] Perhaps the king at that moment recollected a conversation he (King David) had had with God years earlier: *"Who am I, O Lord GOD, and what is my house, that you have brought me thus far?"*[165]

---

[164] 2 Samuel 9:8.
[165] 2 Samuel 7:18.

The orphan's name was Mephibosheth, and he had been summoned by the high king, and hustled away from his exiled home called Lo-debar (translated, "of no value"). Mephibosheth, at the age of five, had lost more than most people do in a lifetime: his father, his grandfather, his home, his wealth, his family status, and the use of his legs. The boy had lived in obscurity for some years, and now was discovered and subpoenaed by the lethal warrior King David.

Mephibosheth, at age five, would have scarcely understood that his family's monarchy had crumbled. He was the third generation of Israel's first monarch, the feted King Saul, and the son of Jonathan a prince of the United Kingdom of Israel. His father was killed at the battle of Mount Gilboa by the hands of the Philistines, and his grandfather, seeing the rout of his army and the deaths of his three sons, fell on his own sword.

Mephibosheth was caught in a web of political expedience; it was common to kill any in a royal lineage that threatened new leadership. His nurse understood the danger the small boy was in, and she was able to help him escape Israel, but in the chaos, there was an accident, and Mephibosheth lost the use of his legs. The boy grew up in exile with no understanding that he was protected under a covenant of grace.

Scripture reveals that King David lived a life of miraculous achievement and meteoric failure. From the historic day when David slung a stone into Goliath's forehead, and promptly decapitated his enemy, David's life was a series of highly honorable and profoundly shameful events. Due to Saul's disobedience, God had conferred leadership on David in a long and protracted affair, as Luke restates in the book of Acts the words of the prophet Samuel.

> *"And when he had removed him, he raised up David to be their king, of whom he testified and said, 'I have found in David the son of Jesse a man after my heart, who will do all my will.'"*[166]

David was under a theocracy, an overlord accountable only to God. David was at times a fugitive himself (before his kingship, and afterward), and would experience jealousy,

---

[166] Acts 13:22.

vengeance, treachery, infidelity, incest, rape, betrayal, murder, duplicity, and conspiracy, and these events would shadow him throughout his life.

King David would indeed walk in *"the valley of the shadow of death.*"[167] He also ascended high mountains, experiencing loyalty, success, love, intimacy, and friendship, as well as a total and unmitigated victory on the battlefield. David was a *rugged* warrior, and yet he was a poet and musician whose praise to God has been a profound source of comfort and encouragement to readers for over 3,000 years.

David's adversity was an outcome of his faithfulness to God, and much of his heartbreaking hardship was a self-inflicted consequence of poor and disobedient decisions. Throughout all of his tumultuous life, David was keenly aware of God's grace, and maintained a passionate and repentant heart. At times David would weep, wholly demoralized; then David fled from Naioth at Ramah, and went to Jonathan, and asked: *"What have I done? What is my guilt? And what is my sin before your father, that he seeks my life?"*[168] Other times he was euphoric: *"And David danced before the LORD with all his might. And David was wearing a linen ephod."*[169]

Like Mephibosheth, David himself was no stranger to exile. He had a rocky relationship with King Saul, who seems to have gone mad, and desired David (his giant killer) to play the harp, which eased his spirit.[170] On occasion, Saul would go into a rage and fling his spear; David or his own son Jonathan were often his targets.[171]

Jonathan, a handsome man and a skilled warrior in his own right, was intensely loyal to David: they were a model of friendship. But Jonathan was also a prince and would fight to the death for his father and family.

Was it the chaos of a tyrant father/king which brought Jonathan and David together, or was it perhaps the fact Jonathan had more than once undermined his father's plans to have David killed? Not many of us have experienced a more profound friendship than what

---

[167] Psalm 23:4.
[168] 1 Samuel 20:1.
[169] 2 Samuel 6:14.
[170] 1 Samuel 16:14-23.
[171] 1 Samuel 19:10.

David had with Jonathan. The prince recognized his divided allegiance, and made a covenant with David, requesting that his comrade would in the event of his death protect his family, and asked:

> *"If I am still alive, show me the steadfast love of the LORD, that I may not die; and do not cut off your steadfast love from my house forever, when the LORD cuts off every one of the enemies of David from the face of the earth.' And Jonathan made a covenant with the house of David, saying, 'May the LORD take vengeance on David's enemies.'"*[172]

Jonathan would indeed die in battle, fighting shoulder to shoulder with his father and brothers against the dreaded Philistines. David would eventually take the crown and unify the kingdom. King David would experience a time of collected power and wealth and extend his kingdom with remarkable success.

In a rare break from war, David, now fully ascended to the kingship, remembers the covenant of grace promised to the house of Jonathan. After years of living in the wilderness, persecuted and hunted by the cursed King Saul, David finally and at times reluctantly becomes king. It was common and strategic for the good of peace and the king's sovereignty to execute any threat to his power and supremacy. Thus, any relative of a deposed leader could be killed. David understood the covenant of grace God had given him, and that he was under the covenant with his old friend Jonathan as the prophet Samuel was inspired to record:

> *"And the king said, 'Is there not still someone of the house of Saul, that I may show the kindness of God to him?' Ziba said to the king, 'There is still a son of Jonathan; he is crippled in his feet.'"*[173]

At the zenith of King David's kingship, David exhibits a surprising amount of grace to the grandson of Saul, and son of his best friend, Jonathan. So, Mephibosheth stands before the high

---

[172] 1 Samuel 20:14-16.
[173] 2 Samuel 9:3.

king, and is awarded all that was promised to his father Jonathan, and more. King David reassures Mephibosheth:

> *"And David said to him, 'Do not fear, for I will show you kindness for the sake of your father Jonathan, and I will restore to you all the land of Saul your father, and you shall eat at my table always.'"*[174]

Mephibosheth has just been granted his life, his family's wealth, and adoption of protection under the new king, but he did not recognize the grace, and responds:

> *"What is your servant, that you should show regard for a dead dog such as I?"*[175]

Have you experienced grace? I meet with students who have memorized Scripture, understand the technical concept of grace, and yet do not know grace, and sadly have never experienced it. Mephibosheth did not get many breaks in his young life, was unaware he was under a covenant of grace, and did not recognize it when it came. When I see grace in very tangible ways, I understand more of what our Lord has done for us.

I was a lousy Boy Scout. I really loved the camping and outdoors, but my young life and mouth were out of control. I was kicked out for swearing, as I found out there weren't any "merit" badges in the Boy Scouts for swearing. In the Boy Scouts, I never got a "un-merit" badge for doing nothing. Christianity is totally different in that you get the most significant "favor" (eternal life in heaven) totally "unmerited."

We can learn a lot of lessons from the world of sport: discipline, teamwork, goal setting. We have one dangerous reoccurring theme in sport that runs completely contrary to God's standard. That is self-sufficiency and meritorious achievement. Grace is so countercultural and hard to recognize, especially to those who identify self-worth with what we can achieve. Do the people that you are discipling understand grace? Have they experienced it? Do you demonstrate it in your life? The best way to teach a principle is to model it, and the best way to understand a principle is to experience it. Have the people you

---

[174] 2 Samuel 9:7.
[175] 2 Samuel 7:8.

have discipled really understood grace? You cannot give away what you do not own.

FOR CONTEMPLATION:

The "covenant of grace" is a legal promise that God will save sinners by grace alone, through faith alone, in Christ alone. Grace is defined as "unmerited favor"; it is the undeserved favor of God at Christ's expense. Scripture teaches that Jesus is the Christ, the Messiah, and Son of God. We by faith enjoy His grace, are children of God, adopted into His family. We cannot earn it!

If you have never experienced even a small amount of grace, it may be hard to recognize a huge amount when it comes your way. It is hard to believe in something that you have never experienced.

- Have you experienced grace? How/when?
- How are you at giving grace?
- Do we have patience with those that have never experienced grace and struggle to understand God's amazing grace?
- As disciple-makers, can we do better at redeploying the countercultural concept of *rugged* grace?

Chapter 17
Rugged Stewardship: *"Come and Share Your Master's Happiness"*: It's Never Too Late

"Remember, you have one life. That's all. You were made for God. Don't waste it."[176]

"The earth is the LORD'S..."[177]

"For it will be like a man going on a journey, who called his servants and entrusted to them his property. To one he gave five talents, to another two, to another one, to each according to his ability. Then he went away. He who had received the five talents went at once and traded with them, and he made five talents more. So also he who had the two talents made two talents more. But he who had received the one talent went and dug in the ground and hid his master's money. Now after a long time the master of those servants came and settled accounts with them. And he who had received the five talents came forward, bringing five talents more, saying, 'Master, you delivered to me five talents; here I have made five talents more.' His master said to him, 'Well done, good and faithful servant. You have been faithful over a little; I will set you over much. Enter into the joy of your master.' And he also who had the two talents came forward, saying, 'Master, you delivered to me two talents; here I have made two talents more.' His master said to him, 'Well done, good and faithful servant. You have been faithful over a little; I will set you over much. Enter into the joy of your master.' He also who had received the one talent came forward, saying, 'Master, I knew you to be a hard man, reaping where you did not sow, and gathering where you scattered no seed, so I was afraid, and I went and hid your talent in the ground. Here you have what is yours.'

---

[176] John Piper, *Don't Waste Your Life, Study Group Version.* Crossways, 2007, p. 13.
[177] Psalm 24:1.

But his master answered him, 'You wicked and slothful servant! You knew that I reap where I have not sown and gather where I scattered no seed? Then you ought to have invested my money with the bankers, and at my coming I should have received what was my own with interest. So take the talent from him and give it to him who has the ten talents. For to everyone who has will more be given, and he will have an abundance. But from the one who has not, even what he has will be taken away. And cast the worthless servant into the outer darkness. In that place there will be weeping and gnashing of teeth.'"[178]

Two things bring back memories of my office in the heart of Scotland. The first is the sound of children playing, and the second, the sad regrets of an old man crying.

Wherever I travel, the sounds of children laughing and playing are remarkably similar. I like to think of play and its beautiful sounds as a universal language of praise. Isn't it interesting that we don't have to teach children to play? In fact, play produces healthy well-being for both children and adults. I like to imagine that the sound of children playing brings God much joy. There are intrinsic dreams that emerge from the hearts of children on the playground. Adventure, teamwork, competition, discovery, and development of new skills emerge. Humans were made in the image and likeness of our Creator. Children love to play, so what must God's play be like?

Sadly, humans are a fallen race, and slaves to sin. Some ugly things emerge from the playground, including selfishness, arrogance, racism, exploitation, cruelness, and hate.

Just beyond an ancient stone wall about 100 yards from my office in central Scotland, sat our village's elementary school. Several times throughout the day when school was in session, I was delighted to hear the sounds of children playing on the playground. I couldn't distinguish their words; it was just muted squeals and laughter.

While lecturing in Pakistan, I overheard some boys playing cricket in the street near where I was staying; for a moment I was back in my office in Scotland. From then on, wherever I travel, I have made it a point to stop and listen to

---

[178] Matthew 25:14-30.

children as they play. The sound of boys and girls skylarking on makeshift playgrounds— whether in a concrete bunker, Western city park, Polynesian ghetto, or refugee camp—always lifts my spirit and reminds me that all over the world, God is being glorified. *"Let the little children come to me and do not hinder them, for to such belongs the kingdom of heaven."*[179]

Another universal sound (and a key to healthy maturity) is the sound of crying. If your office is near a school playground, you will inevitably hear the sound of a child's cry. On one particular day, I heard weeping that did not come from outside my office, but from inside, and the man doing the crying was far older than the children I was used to hearing. It, too, was a form of praise.

Andrew was the typically stoic Scottish gentleman, and in his mid-70's. He had made an appointment with me to discuss the possibility of developing a "youth initiative" in his nearby town. I was intrigued and was looking forward to our meeting, as we had been praying for a spiritual foothold in that particular city. Andrew and I had become acquainted at a couple of civic functions. He was always polite, confident, and self-assured, though he had never shown anything but a passive interest for spiritual things during our brief conversations. His phone call to set up an appointment with me was somewhat of a surprise.

He entered my office and got right to the point. "Steve, I want tae start an initiative to help the older bairns in the village tae ken (know) Christ and grow wi God." His enthusiasm was contagious! I was immediately interested in the project.

Had I read him wrong? My instincts told me something about Andrew had changed, and I was curious about how this reserved elderly gentleman had become so interested in the spiritual welfare of the youth in his town. I was starting to get a sense that this was an entirely new drive in his life, and I wanted to know what lit his fuse. I began cautiously, but noticed sadness starting to slowly flow over him as he described a genuine transformation in his heart.

"Steve, I have been in the kirk (church) aw me life. I go awe the time to the kirk well on Sundays ye ken (you know). I wis even an elder. I even gave tae the offering tae keep up the care of oor kirk, and kent that was dein the right thing for me as a

---

[179] Matthew 19:14.

Christian man de yi ken wit I mean like. I kent God but didne think aboot awdody else. But now I feel God's tellin me time's runnin oot, and I've got tae tell awebody aboot Him, and that heaven and hell are real ye ken wit a mean Steve."

Andrew went on to explain that, about a month earlier, he'd had a mild health scare. He had been lying in bed and doing some rare soul-searching. It was then that: "I did something I wouldne usually dae. I started reading the Bible." said Andrew. He further described skipping to the end of the book of Matthew in the New Testament in an effort to find some reassuring verses about eternity.

Andrew went on, "I could mind o Jesus floating away to heaven, and so, I read Matthew 28, which is a perilous place to start." His going to the Bible for soothing reassurance, an exercise that was supposed to ease his mind, had quite the opposite effect. Jesus's words hit him like a crossbow bolt to the heart, and he encountered the Great Commission. Andrew read: "Go therefore and make disciples..."[180] That's when he started to cry!

"Lad, I have wasted so much time! I winted tae forget aw aboot it, but had to ask masel how many folk had a telt aboot God? I'm ashamed tae answer, 'I couldne think o any in my whole damned life!'"

In between greetin (sobs), he continued. "It wis right there: 'Go and make disciples!' I became sick in ma belly as I kent I had completely ignored the commandment. I have wasted ma life, and its nearly done!"

I gave my newfound brother a hug: something, I'm sure, he wasn't used to receiving from another man, and I held him as he cried some more.

He kept repeating: "So much time. I have wasted so much time!"

It was a bit awkward for both of us as this usually poised man opened up his heart. I can still remember the feel of his bony elbow and shoulder blade that pushed through his old tweed sports coat as I self-consciously tried to comfort him. He did not cry just a few tears. This was no misty-eyed sniffle, but instead it was

---

[180] Matthew 28:19.

154

a profound cry of remorse and regret that came from deep within and shook his lean frame from top to bottom.

As his tears began to dry up, I felt as if I was watching a man come out of a coma. There before me was a real-life Ebenezer Scrooge who had finished his three-ghost haunting.[181] Andrew seemed to have woken from a long, deep spiritual sleep. Seeing the ghost of "Christmas Yet to Come," like Ebenezer, Andrew was crushed by what he saw.

By his own will—or, more likely, the power of the Holy Spirit—Andrew did the rare thing, and took a sober appraisal of his life. He weighed it by God's economy and felt his life had produced very little real eternal value. He was moral, hard-working, and somewhat wealthy, but he had made very little investment in what God values: lives that intently glorify Him. Andrew went on to say: "I didne think that helping folk find God was very important or my responsibility ye ken wit am sayin, Steve."

> "Ye ken wit am sayin, Steve."

It is a rare and brave human who reflects on his life and weighs its worth against the one true value which measures eternally. How unique is it for us to really ask if our life has truly achieved Kingdom purpose, and if we have utilized our talents for making eternity real for those around us?

Most of us go through life with our make-believe scoreboards, fooling ourselves into believing we really have achieved something of value and eternal significance. When we pull off the veneer of everything we hold as important (yes, everything), it doesn't measure up to the worth and rank of worshipping God and helping others know Him.

We play our head games that include rationalizing that: a) Evangelistic-disciple-making is not my "spiritual gift"; b) "I was swamped providing for my family"; c) "When I make enough money, then I'll focus more time on ministry"; or d) "Hey, I'm in charge of the church Easter decorating committee…"

Andrew's story of sleeping through God's Great Commission (to go and make disciples) is not uncommon. Unfortunately, most people never wake up. There is something

---

[181] Charles Dickens, *A Christmas Carol*, 1843.

inside us that was created to worship and serve our Creator, and to encourage others to do the same.

The famous Westminster Shorter Catechism asks and then responds: *"What is the chief end of man?"* The answer? *"To glorify God and to enjoy Him forever."*[182] Surely a large part of "glorifying God" must be participating in His simple, redemptive, unwavering plan of making disciples.

My Scottish friend Andrew did wake up, and then went into overdrive. He decided to make up for lost time in a big, big way, and it was all I could do to keep up with this brother who was twice my age. He became an inspirational but exhausting partner! Very few of Andrew's peers enjoyed his newfound purpose. Unfortunately, he seemed to have pricked many of their consciences, but thankfully many of the young people in his village got to know him, and they fell in love with him.

Sometimes I can come off hard on my friends. Maybe, at times, I push a bit more than is comfortable for them, but I have observed that God seems to get really angry when we waste our lives... *"cast the worthless servant into the outer darkness..."*[183] I never again want to hold in my arms another sobbing person who realized in his last years that he had wasted precious time and his greatest resource—his life. I do not want to waste mine either.

When do we abandon the foundational dreams embedded deep into our hearts for an empty, unsatisfactory life? When do we lose the joy we once had in the playground? The passions, ideas, and sense of adventure we had as children have been pushed back—way back—somewhere into that hard-to-reach, secluded area of our souls.

These desires will sometimes percolate out of our hard hearts and touch us when we least expected them. Once in a while, we may cross paths with a "lion-hearted" Christian that can kindle or rekindle the eternal longing for what only God

---

[182] *Westminster Shorter Catechism, Agreed upon by the Assembly of Divines at Westminster, with the assistance of Commissioners from the Church of Scotland, as a part of the Covenanted University in Religion Betwixt the Churchs of Christ in the Kings of Scotland, Ireland, England, and Ireland.* July 20th, 1648, Question 1.

[183] Matthew 25:30.

fulfills. Many of those deep-seated, larger-than-life longings for some significant purpose may have been crushed on that same playground.

Over time, you may have chased these longings blindly down a wrong road. Your desire for eternal purpose may have been substituted by self-gratification, for things that never really satisfy. Or a worse scenario is when men and women lose the courage to chase God's embedded longings and purpose, and gradually give up on those God-given dreams.

We lose our focus and anesthetize our hunger to all the adventure and joy that this life once promised. If we are not careful, a measure of cynicism is easily formed at the gateway of our hearts, to guard us against the disillusionment of unfulfilled dreams. We then miss the adventure we could have had in serving God.

Andrew woke up and started looking for a deeper meaning. His pilgrimage began late. Jesus promises that He is the "abundant life." Those things we chased on the playground of our youth are found only in Him. When we enter into a life of loving and genuinely knowing God, we start to enjoy what He loves, and share what He has to share. We realize that all is His, and we are to responsibly utilize all we possess for Kingdom purposes. The journey is painful, and God will strip us of many things that we may think are important, only to help us determine what value, fulfillment, and success genuinely are.

We need not walk alone. Aren't you also glad God has given us brave men and women who are also journeying with Him, helping us to love and know Him? Can you be one of those guides, and help others on their journey?

In my role as a football team chaplain, I often find myself hugging a player that has just lost a grandparent. This is usually the first significant death in his life. The pain and loss are deep and painful. At these points I often ask my players if their grandparent was a spiritual person. The athlete regularly looks at me with searching, tear-stained eyes, and frequently expresses that he's not sure. It never occurred to him to have a spiritual conversation with his dear grandparents. His grandparent may have gone to church, but he never had a spiritual conversation with his grandson.

When you see the profound loss athletes experience, you understand the remarkable significance the older person had in their lives. I find myself saddened that the grandparent did not take more time to spiritually disciple the young man. Young people are rarely skilled at expressing the appreciation they have for the older people in their lives, but when you hold a giant football star who is crying on the practice field, you understand the remarkable influence they had on the grandchild.

It has been a long time since that first meeting with Andrew. I haven't lived in that little village for some time, and Andrew has since gone to be with the Lord. Yet, he was a mentor who discipled me. When I hear the sound of children playing in any part of the world, I often remember my old office and that first meeting with Andrew. The times when I feel like taking the foot off the gas and coasting spiritually for just a few blocks, I often think of my Scottish friend: of holding him; of his shaking, sobbing, remorseful tears. I also remember how he pressed hard in the last chapter of his life. It reminds me to: "keep going, fat boy; let's see if you can do a little bit for the Kingdom. Let's try to love your heavenly Father more, know Him better, and serve Him more." Andrew helps me want to participate in God's grand plan of making disciples.

POSTSCRIPT:

As I drove to a church for a speaking engagement in the highlands of Scotland, I brought along a new friend. We started to talk about his family, and then his business. He explained to me how he became wealthy during a particularly unprofitable time in the United Kingdom. He described how he built his company through hard work, how he sold the right products in an evolving market, and how he developed a shrewd management style.

I exclaimed, "Wow, God has really blessed you."

My friend somewhat proudly replied, "No, this is my business, and I have blessed myself."

As we become disciples of Christ, we have a major transformational shift when we realize that all we naturally possess and acquire over a lifetime (skills, belongings, finances, education, family, work ethic, health, time, etc.) are God's. We are not owners, but rather stewards, of all we possess. We come to appreciate that all we have has been entrusted to us by our loving Father for a higher purpose.

> *"This is how one should regard us, as servants of Christ and stewards of the mysteries of God. Moreover, it is required of stewards that they be found trustworthy."*[184]

Mature Christians understand they are servants of God and have been endowed with a wide array of gifts to enjoy and to utilize responsibly for God's glory. Our entire life is in a stewardship relationship with our gracious and heavenly Father, and we will be held accountable for the talents lovingly bestowed upon us.

> *Jesus teaches us we are to utilize whatever talent we have for multiplying His kingdom wisely.*

Jesus teaches us we are to utilize whatever talent we have for multiplying His Kingdom wisely. We also start to understand that our talents are not limited merely to our finances; everything we possess is God's.

As we start to grasp the concept of *rugged* stewardship, we give up the foolish idea that we are the masters of our life. Scripture tells us that we are accountable to God for all He has given us. Jesus reminds us of this in His famous "Parable of the Talents" and the "Parable of the Minas."[185]

Jesus taught in the "Parable of the Talents" (a "talent" in the first century was a tremendous amount of money) that God will bestow upon us certain gifts. We are to strategically implement these talents for God's glory and Kingdom impact. What is our motivation for using all we have for Kingdom purposes? Will we hear God say:

> *"His master said to him, 'Well done, good and faithful servant. You have been faithful over a little; I will set you over much. Enter into the joy of your master.'"*[186]

---

[184] 1 Corinthians 4:1, 2.
[185] Matthew 25:14-30; Luke 19:12-27.
[186] Ibid.

To please and displease God is a powerfully, motivating idea. It is a deep-seated force in every human life to *do all for the glory of God.*[187] Sadly, sin often obscures that force.

To think that trying to utilize what God has given me can actually "please" Him is a beautiful concept. Not only do I get the fantastic experience of pleasing the Creator of the Universe, He encourages us to share in our Master's happiness.

Are we teaching others that obedience to God and His commission is simply our duty? Or are we reveling in the joy that we can have when we enter into a pleasing relationship with Him? God wants to share His happiness with you. Will you allow Him to? When we realize we are stewards of our very lives, we are free to enjoy and appreciate all we possess in more satisfying ways.

FOR CONTEMPLATION:

I used to think Christians who were not engaged in discipleship were selfish, but now I think they just don't know how rewarding it is.

- What Christian entering heaven would not want to hear from Jesus: "Well done, good and faithful servant! You have been faithful with a few things; I will put you in charge of many things. Come and share your master's happiness!"
  - o In what ways have you been a good and faithful servant?
- Do you feel the pleasure of God? *"Come and share your Master's happiness."*
- How can you encourage older people to be intentional about their disciple-making in their grandchildren and the lives of younger people?
  - o Is it ever too late to make disciples?

---

[187] John 15:1-8.

Chapter 18
Rugged Legacy: The Ripple Effect, the Life I Touch… Will Touch Another

"Truly, truly, I say to you, whoever believes in me will also do the works that I do; and greater works than these will he do, because I am going to the Father."[188]

"The life that I touch for good or ill will touch another life, and that in turn another, until who knows where the trembling stops or in what far place my touch will be felt."[189]

Legacy: something received from an ancestor or predecessor or from the past.[190]

Speaking at a pastors' conference during another trip to Cambodia, I was given the option to travel the eight-hour journey from Phnom Penh to Angkor Wat by bus, or I could make the trip on a rented motorcycle. The only dilemma for the motorcycle trip was that I had to travel through an area that was still marginally controlled by the ruthless Khmer Rouge regime, an administration that had, decades earlier, slaughtered millions of Cambodians.

My friend Amos just shrugged when I asked how dangerous it would be. He said: "Ha-ha, you should be fine, just don't run into the Khmer Rouge or Pol Pot." So, I chose to take the motorcycle north to meet with the pastors.

It was the rainy season, and the roads were at times barely manageable unless you are driving a dirt bike. At one point, the Mekong River had burst its banks, and I had to haul my little motorcycle onto an old dugout canoe, and float over a couple of miles of flooded roads and rice paddies, leaving the stranded trucks and buses far behind me. The sun was scorching, and the streets at times were a bog. I watched the locals

---

[188] John 14:8-12.
[189] Frederick Beuchner, *The Hungering Dark*, 1985, p. 292.
[190] Merriam Webster Dictionary.

ride, and slowly got the hang of maneuvering the giant, flooded potholes, but the people and the scenery were beautiful.

Some children, selling gas in coke bottles on the side of the road, gave me a stunned look when I asked them to "fill-er-up!" Big, mud-splattered white guys touring on little rented motorcycles was indeed a novelty.

I saw a lot of hardworking people in subsistence living, coaxing their land into producing enough food for them and their families to survive. On a small detour, I was able to play with children at a beautiful Christian orphanage. Many of those children had lost limbs to the evils of unexploded land mines. Fifty years after they were armed and concealed underground, the mines continue to arbitrarily take a cruel toll on the children who wander onto them.

Thankfully, the Khmer Rouge was not to be found during my journey to the ancient city of Angkor Wat.

It may seem like naive speculation to some, but on those quiet nights when my mind drifts back to Cambodia, I ask myself: "What suffering might have been prevented if someone had led Pol Pot to Jesus?"

For that matter, I ask myself: "What suffering might have been prevented if any evil dictator had encountered the Prince of Peace and had been transformed by His grace?"

Then I seem to automatically ask, "What evil might have occurred if I had not heard of Jesus from my old high school coach?" Finally, I ask, "What potential evil can be avoided if we reach that poor, disturbed junior high kid for Jesus?" We are laying a foundation for our grandchildren's future, for good or bad. What might that look like?

I hope I don't sound like I have a "Messiah complex" (the sad state of mind in which an individual holds a belief that he is solely responsible for the salvation of others). I recognize the best I can do is try to be committed to God and be obedient to His calling.

Do not be overcome by evil, but overcome evil with good.[191]

---

[191] Romans 12:21.

I understand that it is the Holy Spirit's job to convert. Though I can't save anyone, it is my responsibility to have spiritual conversations, to help those in need, to try and build into the lives that God puts into my sphere of influence, to do my best to *"overcome evil with good."*

Though my backside was a bit tender, the long trip to Angkor Wat was a great adventure. I was 24 hours early for the pastors' conference, and excited at the opportunity this presented to explore the famous ancient temples. Rolling up to the city gates, I was immediately met by a chaotic squad of hawkers (guides) and an enormous army of beggar children who all converged on me like flies on dung. I was sunburned, tired, and covered in road dust. All I wanted was a shower, a bed, and one of those beautiful Cambodian meals.

The guides were a little bemused to see a foreigner turning up on a rented motorcycle instead of a tour bus. Still, after they recovered from their initial shock, they started pressing in on me, competing for my attention. The children, meantime, wanted me to buy them a bag of chips or a bottle of water. The guides were all driving those crazy little motorized rickshaws called tuk-tuks, and each boasted that he was the best tour guide in the historic city.

Choosing a guide can be tricky, and I hated to disappoint any of them. One guide really stood out; his tuk-tuk had big letters across the side, saying, "Dr. Smart." I liked the look of the driver, so I asked Dr. Smart to suggest a clean, cheap hotel.

He was easy-going and funny. His English was barely understandable, but I couldn't hold that against him. I had lived and worked in Oxford, England, for several years, and one of the professors at the city's famous university told me that my English was also barely comprehensible.

Dr. Smart recommended an excellent hotel and suggested that he could give me a tour of the fantastic ruins of the historic temples in the morning. He also proposed a great restaurant. What could be nearer and dearer to my heart than that?

I told my new "guide" that I also had a massive headache from being in the heat all day, and did he know where I could get something for it? He suggested a massage. I love Asia for many reasons, but massages are at the top of the list! I brightened at the idea, and said: "Yes, that sounds great!"

My new friend boasted that he knew all the best places to get a massage and went on to list about five different types of massages, none of which I could understand. He tried again, a little slower this time. With a sly grin, he asked me if I wanted a "boom-boom massage?"

"Boom-boom? What is a boom-boom massage?"

He looked a little embarrassed, and replied: "You know, boom-boom," and did a little gyration with his hips. Alarmed, I responded: "No! No! No! No boom-boom massage! I'm a good Christian man. No, boom-boom!"

He laughed and said he would get me a good "'Christian massage.' No problem. No boom-boom."

I was a little relieved, while at the same time, wondered what a "Christian massage" was. I checked into the hotel recommended by Dr. Smart, and it wasn't too bad. I pondered what percentage he got from the hotel for sending my custom their way.

As I entered my room, I watched the little lizards scatter. (Lizards, I learned, are useful because they eat the spiders!) My shower was hot, which was a pleasant surprise. I changed and returned to the lobby, where my trusty guide was waiting for me. Dr. Smarts' motorized tuk-tuk was a welcome sight after being on a muddy motorcycle all day. He took me to a restaurant where the meal was fantastic, and I started thinking that I had indeed picked the right man to guide me around northern Cambodia. After dinner, Dr. Smart was excited to take me to my much-needed massage.

His rickshaw was a small, whiney crate, but it was nice not to have to maneuver my motorcycle and my fatigued body around an unknown city. Dr. Smart weaved through the traffic like a Formula One driver and did his best to miss the flooded potholes. It was dark, but there were lights everywhere, covering the old buildings. Dr. Smart pointed out some interesting sights, and then slowly passed by a dozen girls dressed in strange, colorful gowns, and wearing lots of gaudy makeup.

The women were sitting together in an open storefront, each flashing a fake smile and blank stare. It broke my heart, realizing that underneath all that makeup, many of them were just young girls barely into their teens. My guide looked back at me, smiling, and said: "Here boom-boom massage." Thankfully Dr. Smart lived up to his name and heeded my dirty look. He lost his naughty grin and kept going. "Your massage is far away." So off we went, leaving the city, then passing through a village before the houses thinned out, and finally, we were in a rainforest. (When did we stop calling it a jungle?)

My excitement slowly turned to apprehension with every kilometer we traveled away from the city. It was getting darker and quieter. Finally, we turned down a gloomy footpath, and approached a small, unlit shack.

With a satisfied smile, Dr. Smart turned and said: "Here we are. Very good massage for you." We got out of his tuk-tuk. I felt uneasy, like I was trespassing, but Dr. Smart pounded on the door until, to my surprise, it opened just a crack. There was a brief exchange of words in Khmer, and then Dr. Smart steered a small, mysterious person from the house into the rickshaw I had just vacated.

I told my guide: "Hey, they are obviously closed. No problem, just take me back to the hotel."

Dr. Smart replied, a little too hurriedly for my liking, with: "They are open, they are open. Just wait here, I will be back!" And with that, Dr. Smart and the mysterious person, who I think was a lady, sped away.

There is nothing like being stranded in a jungle in a country ravaged by violence to motivate you to you pray. First, I asked God to forgive me for being an idiot and letting myself get stranded in the middle of the bush. Then I asked for help! "Yikes, God, I could use a big angel right about now!" After my short but very intense talk with my Father, I tried to hide my money and passport on my body, which is pretty hard to do when you are dressed in shorts, polo shirt, and flip-flops.

As I stood on a dark path in front of the shack, the sound and shape of Dr. Smart's rickshaw faded and then disappeared altogether. I strained to listen for any sign of life, but all I could hear was the sound of my heart beating. On the one hand I was thinking how dumb I was to get into this predicament, yet on the other hand a part of me was thinking this was indeed one of the coolest adventures I had ever had!

After a few minutes of anxious waiting, the sound of Dr. Smart's unmistakable vehicle again became audible through the trees. I imagined seeing five guys hanging off the tuk-tuk, waving swords and guns. I looked for a place to run, or possibly a weapon, but mainly, I kept asking God to help.

Finally, Dr. Smart came into view, and to my relief, his only passenger was a shadowy-looking man. I figured I could take these guys, or at least I could outrun them if needed. My guide pulled up, jumped out of his tuk-tuk, and led his passenger into the small house. I admired the way Dr. Smart took gentle care of the man who was now silhouetted by the moonlight. I could feel my heart rate dropping and the adrenaline draining from my body. But I still didn't really get what was happening.

I was still wondering what I had gotten myself into when Dr. Smart (looking quite satisfied with himself and wearing his perpetual reassuring grin) gleefully invited me into the building. When the mysterious passenger finally switched on a light, I was shocked to see that his face had been horribly disfigured. Slowly it dawned on me why their house had been in darkness. The man, and most likely also, the woman, were blind. This man had probably sometime in his life stepped on a landmine.

The house was just a two-roomed hut. I was buoyed to see a large cross hanging on a wall. My guide had brought me to a blind Christian masseuse. What an unexpected surprise! Dr. Smart, acting as a translator, introduced the man as Piseth. I was asked to lie down on the massage table, which was covered in clean white sheets. Piseth turned on a small, battered CD player, and started playing a beautiful Cambodian version of Amazing Grace.

My masseuse must not have been used to Americans, especially former football players, because when he grabbed my shoulders, he seemed astonished by my size, and gave a grunt of amazement. I knew exactly what he meant! Then he started to chuckle, and so did I.

His hands were strong and professional. He worked the kinks out of my neck and shoulders, and kneaded my back. When Piseth started massaging my hamstrings, he let out an amazed, "whhaaaaa!" It must have been the most prominent rump he had ever worked on! We both started laughing. His hands were powerful, and he knew just how far to work the muscles. He definitely put the vise on me, but he never crossed the line into absolute agony, though he came very close!

It was apparent he was a well-trained professional. He knew what he was doing, and by the end of the session, I felt like a new man. Piseth touched me physically and had encouraged me spiritually. It was an excellent massage, and a delightful adventure.

When it was time to go, I paid him. He then handed me a small piece of printed paper with an image of the cross. I realized I had just been given an evangelistic tract. I was so humbled and blessed that Piseth was trying to tell me about his Savior.

I asked Dr. Smart to tell my blind evangelist that I, too, loved Jesus. It did not seem to translate very well, so I took Piseth's hand and made the sign of the cross on his heart, and then he took my hand and made the sign of the cross on his heart, too. We both teared up as Piseth patted my shoulder. We said our goodbyes, I climbed back into the little rickshaw, and as we motored away, I watched the light in the house turn off.

The small tract that Piseth had given me was written in Khmer, and Dr. Smart tried but was not really able to provide me with an adequate translation. I learned at the pastors' conference that Piseth was from an offshoot of a non-government organization that was established 100 years ago by a German pastor-missionary, Ernest Christoffel, and a Catholic mission society. They had partnered to help victims of blindness and, later, those injured by land mines.

Piseth had been abandoned by his family. Later, Cambodian Christians, who were also blind, had brought him to their mission. They shared the love of Christ with him, and over time, discipled him. He was now working and sharing Christ with others. The ripple effect from Jesus' discipleship plan reached the marginalized a continent away.

There are a lot of people attempting to alleviate pain and injustice in this world. The problems and answers are complicated. Sex slavery, beggars, addictions, and inequality have been around for millennia. There have been all too few solutions. A heart transformed by Jesus is the only lasting answer that I have found for breaking the cycle of evil. It is the

Apostle Paul's simple rule of supply and demand: *"Do not be overcome by evil, but overcome evil with good."*[192]

If you reach someone for Christ, he transforms from evil to good. It is incredible to think we can participate in God's plan to touch a life. A principle that can create a ripple effect that will last for eternity.

> *If you reach someone for Christ, he transforms from evil to good.*

When my prayers go to Cambodia, I often think of how blessed I was to meet Dr. Smart and Piseth. I know that the Cambodian Christian population is growing, but what are the odds of getting to meet a Christian masseuse in the middle of the jungle!

I often think what our world would be like if people like Ernest Christoffel and many other *rugged* Christians had not responded to the Great Commission? Ernest Christoffel is long dead, but his work has had a lasting legacy, which has taken on many new and exciting forms.

What amazing adventures does God have for those who are obedient to His calling? What might your legacy to the Great Commission look like in 100 years? You may never know, until you get to heaven, but we can take heart that Jesus promised: *"greater works than these will he do, because I am going to the Father."*[193]

POSTSCRIPT:

A ripple effect happens when dropping an object into the water, and the waves are incrementally followed outward.

John, the youngest of the twelve disciples, gives us a candid glimpse of Jesus's interaction with the twelve, hours before His crucifixion. The disciples may have sensed their education was about to climax, and they were still seeking more. Jesus had washed their feet and predicted His betrayal and Peter's denial. Jesus goes on to comfort His disciples, telling them:

> *"Let not your hearts be troubled. Believe in God; believe also in me. In my Father's house are many rooms. If it*

---

[192] Romans 12:21.
[193] John 14:12.

were not so, would I have told you that I go to prepare a place for you?"[194]

The disciple Thomas, who was always the inquirer, asked Jesus: *"Lord, we do not know where you are going. How can we know the way?"*[195]

Jesus gives arguably the most precise and definitive answer to the nature of His mission: *"I am the way, and the truth, and the life. No one comes to the Father except through me."*[196]

Now Philip was still confused, and seeking clarity, asks Jesus: *"Lord, show us the Father, and it is enough for us."*[197] To this, Jesus gently explains: *"Believe me that I am in the Father and the Father is in me, or else believe on account of the works themselves."*[198]

Then Jesus casts a remarkable vision/challenge to His dear disciples when He says: *"Truly, truly, I say to you, whoever believes in me will also do the works that I do; and greater works than these will he do, because I am going to the Father."*[199]

How can we do greater works than Jesus did? Jesus' meaning is that we will do more, not in nature, but in abundance. Jesus' mission was to save the world. His plan was to nurture disciples to execute His objectives. This is precisely what Jesus predicted, and is precisely what happened!

After Pentecost, His close-knit team of disciples started to disperse and yet, through the power of the Holy Spirit (promised by Jesus in John 14-18), the world was never the same again. We are still feeling the effects, and you can be an extension to Jesus' "Master plan," and help reach a generation that you may never meet.

If you don't like adventure, don't get involved in making disciples. Jumping out of a plane produces a fantastic adrenaline rush. Sailing solo through a storm and coming out the other end with your sailboat intact is thrilling, and yet there is nothing more adventurous than serving Jesus. The buzz lasts for eternity.

---

[194] John 14:1, 2.
[195] John 14:5.
[196] John 14:6.
[197] John 14:8.
[198] John 14:11.
[199] John 14:12.

The root of the word "adventure" means "a thing about to happen." It is where we get the Christmas word "advent." Whenever we serve Christ, we get an adventure, and each adventure is never the same; as the Old Testament says: *"They are new every morning."*[200] Sometimes it takes a long time to understand, but when we serve Jesus, something unexpected usually arrives, an eternal escapade as recorded by Paul in his letter to the church in Philippi: *"for it is God who works in you, both to will and to work for his good pleasure."*[201]

FOR CONTEMPLATION:

I used to think that winning a Super Bowl championship ring would be my greatest accomplishment, but now I realize that there are few things you get to bring to heaven. However, whatever I do in Jesus' name has significance, as put forth so brilliantly by Jesus' disciple and Gospel writer Matthew: *"Whoever gives one of these little ones even a cup of cold water because he is a disciple, truly, I say to you, he will by no means lose his reward."*[202]

- In the process of making disciples, what adventure might come your way, and what legacy might you leave for the next generation?
- What impact can you make that will outlive you?
- Do you know that God's rewards last forever?

---

[200] Lamentations 3:23.
[201] Philippians 2:13.
[202] Matthew 10:42.

Chapter 19
Rugged Marriage and Family:
"But as for Me and My House..."

In Los Angeles, at a Super Bowl party, I was sitting on a couch, a bit sullen. I was watching several of my old teammates on the Chicago Bears crush the Patriots. My heart was thrilled for the players and the coaching staff, but it was tough not being there. I had been released from the team and then the Los Angeles Rams after a career-ending knee surgery. The good news was, I was sitting next to a cute blond that assuaged my disappointment. I married her! For over thirty years, I have watched my old teammates wave that Chicago Bears Super Bowl ring. Yet if I had not been injured and gone to Los Angeles, I would not have been sitting next to that blond. I look at my wedding ring, think of my three children, and wonder at God's providence. Would I trade my wedding ring from Michelle for a Super Bowl ring? Well—some days—but not many!

Over the years, I have been discipled, and have discipled many *rugged* men and women. The discipleship lifestyle is wonderful. God has put some remarkable, transformative characters in my life. Yet, nothing has been more transformative than my *rugged* marriage and *rugged* family.

Rudyard Kipling wrote: *"What do they know of England who only England know?"*[203] What he was saying is that travel will give you perspective. You will understand your land and culture better after experiencing other places. Travel is such a privilege and provides a good sense of perspective. It has contributed so much to my own education.

On my first trip to India, I was struggling to pack my bags. I was to preach the two Sundays while in the country, and I felt I needed to pack some formal shoes. Paul, a good friend and the pioneer of sports ministry in India, had asked me to disciple some of his leaders: in particular, a national soccer player and coach named Francis. My friend Paul always looked a bit more formal than the Westerners at our international planning meetings. My training is usually with athletes, so formal wear is

---

[203] Rudyard Kipling, *The English Flag*, p. 189.

often not needed. My big feet require big shoes. Dress shoes weigh a lot, and I could use that precious space for gifts and books to give to my friends. I had an internal debate: should I, or shouldn't I, bring my dress shoes? Finally, I relented and threw them in the bag.

After the long flight, I was picked up by a smiling Francis, and taken to a local hostel. I barely seemed to close my eyes when Francis was knocking at my door, "Good morning, brother, time to go." I sat on the back of his little motorcycle, and zoomed through the streets of Chennai, dressed for church. The sermon outline was tumbling through my mind, and I was pleased I made an effort and packed my good shoes. A half-hour later, now fully awake and enjoying the rush of new sights, smells, and sounds of southern India, we arrived. As we pulled up to the old church, I had to laugh. The entrance was filled with a sea of sandals and flip-flops. No one wore shoes in the church! To wear shoes in Francis' church was seen to be disrespectful. I had to grin; my paradigm had shifted again. I preached in my socks.

The young Indian Christians I met were both committed and intelligent. Their vision for India was inspiring, and their strategy was practical. Their hope and dreams were on a grand scale, which encouraged my faith.

My Western sensibilities were again challenged when I slowly realized the majority of these young Indian leaders had an "arranged marriage." This realization (another paradigm shift) has actually encouraged my marriage over the years. Having an arranged marriage, usually chosen through mutual agreement by the parents, seemed so alien to me.

After building trust and mutual respect with Francis and his cadre of Christian leaders, I had to inquire about their marriage system. I asked Francis and the other young men and women, if they felt cornered or coerced by the arranged marriage. "No, we like the system," many replied. I asked if they wished they had a "love marriage." One woman said, "A love marriage is a silly title because our 'arranged marriages' are also based on love." I asked, "How could you be in love after only meeting someone a few times?" She answered, "Because we choose to love. Love is not like a cloud that floats over some people, and perhaps unintentionally floats away. Love is a choice, and we choose to love the man or woman that God—through our parents—has given us." I asked, still a bit mystified, "How much time did you spend with your spouse before the wedding?" Answers varied from "several chaperoned walks" to "one luncheon with the families."

Most arranged marriages involve parental participation. At a particular age, the parents start to look for a match. This happens through family and extended networks. The families will look at the values, personalities, and virtues of the children. Yet, the notion of finding a "perfect match" based on "chemistry" is foreign to many Indians. This "perfect match" idea has been brought to us over the past fifty years by dating services that exploit lonely people. Not all my Indian friends have arranged marriages, but the ones that do, trust their parents, and trust God's institution of marriage. I have often heard them say, "Our parents have known us longer than we have known ourselves; they have wisdom we have not yet acquired. They will make godly decisions."

Healthy arranged marriage is like any other healthy marriage. You choose to love each other. My Indian friends do not talk in terms of "good chemistry" or "feelings." There is an expectancy that love will grow. Expectations for intimacy start lower in an "arranged marriage"; they understand it takes time for love to grow. The hope that love grows with time relieves disappointments when the honeymoon wears off.

Like many Western marriages, "arranged marriage" couples learn to assimilate the spouse's wants, preferences, and dreams, and make them their own. Couples learn to make decisions together; they learn to share their intimate feelings. They explore each other mentally, physically, socially, spiritually, and learn to meet each other's desires. To choose to love a spouse is a *rugged* choice of your will powered by the Holy Spirit, in alignment to the Scripture.

Yes, not every marriage in India is ideal. Some marriages are arranged out of convenience, financial, or caste obligation. Some women are subjugated by tyrannical husbands. Yet statistics point out Indian marriages are more satisfying than their Americans counterparts. The divorce rate in India is 1 in 100, arguably the lowest in the world.[204]

Now I am under no illusion that this book is going to change a trend for arguably six billion people on how they will pick a spouse. Nor would I want to, though there are times when I would like to choose the right spouse for my own children. Reversely, I thank God that my father did not pick my spouse: he would have chosen for me an excellent pole dancer. Yet, when I see the way my dear friend Francis has reflexively chosen to love God by cultivating his beautiful family, it gives me hope. There is no magic spell of falling into or out of love. Emotions come and go; there is no enchanted chemistry needed to cultivate a beautiful marriage.

Christians are aware that marriage is a sacramental institute designed by God.[205] You choose to honor and invest in the spiritual and legally binding commitment. Marriage is built on the foundation of dedication and duty rather than passion. Romance and passion are lovely, but they are not foundational to marriage. Instead, they become byproducts of God's perfect institution.

Much of Western society talks much about self-realization, but little of discipline. Romance is an ethereal feeling. Many worldly people think, if the feelings dry up, you can simply "if you are lucky" find another person that will give you a romantic experience.

I often read from Christian writers that marriage is not about "*self-fulfillment*" or "*self-realization*." I understand what they are saying, and we are not to guide our lives on tabloid or pop psychology. Your spouse is not a product to merely satisfy your innate needs.

On the surface, I seem to be a nice guy, but my marriage is a *revealing* and shocking mirror to my soul: a reflection which quickly exposes the depth of my sin. Often, I don't like what I see; neither does Michelle. Nothing has given me more "*self-realization*" than my marriage and family. I have *realized* that my capacity for selfishness is ashamedly high. What seems counterintuitive is, my "*self-fulfillment*" has been satisfied in my

---

[204] George Monger, *Marriage Customs of the World: From Henna to Honeymoons*, p. 159.
[205] Genesis 2:23.

dying to self, serving God, and nurturing our family. Most of my dissatisfaction has risen from my selfishness and sin. God has used my marriage and family to disciple me. In light of our marriage, I have learned that contrary to my intuition, putting Michelle, and later my family, before me, is a great and deep joy.

Over the past fifteen years, I have watched Francis grow and develop his church sports ministry. We have spent much time eating on Francis' floor in his home. I have watched him honor his young wife, Bagia, and cultivate his family while raising his wonderful boys. I feel like an uncle to those young men. Francis has eaten many meals with us and stayed at our home several times. He has also observed the way I treat Michelle and watched our family grow. Yes, we live in two unique and dissimilar cultures. Still, the Biblical principles of honoring our wives and dying to self are universal. We have both grown and have been transformed by committing to our wives, families, and the institution of marriage.

Rugged Hospitality

"Choose this day whom you will serve... But as for me and my house, we will serve the LORD.'"[206]

What would it be like to be married to Joshua or be his children? They certainly must have been *rugged*. Joshua's clarion call is a famous Bible verse that hangs on many Christians' walls. To the Israelites, Joshua was sending a challenge to a total commitment to serve God. He drew a line, and challenged them to commit, *"Whom will you serve?"* Joshua not only swore himself to the service of the Lord, but he also pledged the *"house."* He was promising not only his heart and life, but his entire family, to serve the living God. God gave many of us a family for a purpose. Sometimes our most precious gifts can be our worst idols.

I have a coach's heart; I love finding a player's talents and putting him in the right position for success. More importantly, I love recognizing people's talents, and putting them is a position to build the body of Christ. Most of this chapter so far has been about how a sacrificial marriage will help us understand and love

---

[206] Joshua 24:15.

God and our family members more. Marriage itself disciples us. I want to turn now to how your marriage and family will affect others. If you have a healthy marriage full of *rugged* commitment, you are a rare and blessed breed. A healthy, robust marriage is a great gift—a gift entrusted to you by God. Your "talents" are also a great responsibility. If you have been blessed to have a spouse and family, use that gift in your disciple-making.

> *If you have a healthy marriage full of rugged commitment, you are a rare and blessed breed.*

Jesus teaches us stewardship in the "Parable of the Talents."[207] A "talent" is a metaphor for any gifting you may possess. That may include assets, intelligence, health, possessions, marriage, and family. The heart of this parable is, use it or lose it. We are endowed with talents commensurate to our capabilities. Jesus teaches us: "To one servant five talents, to another two, and to another one talent (a talent was a sizable sum of money, arguably millions)." The parable reminds us that we have an essential responsibility to use our "talent" wisely.

So, I ask, why don't more people engage their family in the discipleship process? Our family priorities will always be a difficult tightrope to walk. Besides salvation, my family is my most precious gift I have. Nurturing my family is a prerequisite to my ministry to others. My wife and children know they are more important than any other ministry I have. I love my family so much, if I am not careful, my family can become an idol. I always have to check my motives and continue to reformulate in my mind what is the purpose of family, and what are my priorities. Is my family about my gratification, and a trophy to put on display? Or am I nurturing my family to be healthy and *rugged* Christians for the Kingdom of God? If I treat my wife and children as idols, will they not continue to model the cycle of idolatry? Many parents in my generation, which are famously known as "helicopter parents" (hovering over their children), continue to make their families idols under the guise of being great parents. Our first discipleship is to our family. Do we model that our ministry is more important than our family? Likewise, do we model that our family is more important than our

---

[207] Matthew 25:14-30.

love and devotion to God? Christians will always walk a fine line between engaging our "talents" for the glory of God or worshiping our "talents." I need to remind myself that my greatest family memories have included serving God together side by side.

We desperately need *rugged* family models that understand sacrifice. Paul stresses that those in leadership responsibilities must be persons of hospitality.[208] In first century Middle Eastern culture, hospitality was a fine art. We are to demonstrate and embody our love for God by opening up our homes to the people we disciple.

Again, we will always have to examine our motives. Are we glorifying God? Or under the guise of glorifying God, are we looking for our own glory? I know of a leadership couple from our local church whose family had stopped attending Sunday morning services. When they were asked, "Where have you guys been? We miss you," they admitted, "Our family spends Sunday mornings cleaning; we want our house perfect before we host our evening church small group."

Since I was fifteen, I was, for the most part, on my own. I was not homeless; I just moved to different houses. I stayed with my mom until she was too sick to take care of my young sister and me. My sister and I stayed with my dad and his girlfriend (later wife) and her two kids. My high school coach wanted me to be eligible, and arranged for me to stay in the district, so I stayed at my teammates' homes. They were all kind to give me, an undisciplined teenager, a place to sleep.

The two most authentic examples of discipling/hospitality I experienced were at my friend Mark's grandmother's house, and my friend Russ' home.

Mark's grandmother's name was Gener (short for Genevieve). She was an amazing woman who opened her home to so many of us kids that came from divorced homes who were looking for a bit of stability. She rarely locked the door, and she lived on the route to our high school. We had an open invitation to come into her kitchen and have some chocolate chip cookies, day or night.

On the way home from a workout, Mark invited me to his grandmother's house. We were going out that night, and

---

[208] 1 Timothy 3:1-7; Titus 1:5-9; 1 Peter 5:1-4.

being a sweaty mess, we hit the shower in her basement. As an extension of the locker room, Mark and I started snapping towels at each other naked. Gener, who had just come home from work, came down to the basement to see what all the noise was about. To my horror, she caught Mark and me in the buff. She just laughed, ran upstairs, and asked us if we were hungry. She never mentioned it again and made me feel like I was part of the family.

Gener never read a "how-to" discipleship book in her life. Still, she embodied a sweet blend of both Biblical heroes Mary and Martha. Her house was spotless and organized. She also had an artistic flare. Often Michelle and I, while organizing our home, will ask, "How would Gener decorate that?" Her faith was pure and straightforward, and we were all attracted to her devotion. Her conversation would easily flow from birds in her trees to God's beautiful handiwork. There was a lot of laughter. She lost her husband to cancer, and modeled happy, hard, cheerful labor as she cared for plants, almost until she died, at our local florist.

If I was not at Mark's grandma's house, I was eating dinner at Russ' parents' house. I was very timely; I always just happened to visit near the dinner hour. I was met with a cheerful smile from Mama Graham. Russ' brothers and sister were still around, and happy to share a pillow with me as we watched sports together on television. This was one of the first models of a loving, nurturing family that I saw. Papa Graham was always full of wisdom, and happy to open the Bible and give me some well-needed guidance. Their prayers were genuine and simple. When Papa Graham asked me to pray at their dinner table, I felt a metaphysical validation that I was loved and welcomed.

Like so many, I did not have a model for a Christian home life. These families were a lifeline and an excellent example of our future hospitality. My home was full of anger and swearing; what I remember most from Mama Graham's and Gener's house were laughter and prayers.

POSTSCRIPT:

"Only one thing is necessary..."

178

While writing this chapter, I was explaining to a dear friend how marriage can truly refine us and shape our relationship with God. He reminded me that he was at a breaking point, after going through a particularly rough marital patch. After a particularly ugly argument with his wife, he went upstairs misty-eyed, and threw himself on his bed, empty and hurt. My friend went on to say, "At that point, I had a simple and profound breakthrough. I yelled out to God, 'Okay, I give up. My wife is not going to fulfill who I am. Only You, Father, can do that.'"

The Holy Spirit drew my friend's mind to Jesus' encounter with Mary and Martha. Jesus had brought his disciples to be guests at their home. Martha was busy preparing to serve Jesus and the guests. Mary sat at Jesus' feet. An upset Martha encourages Jesus to tell Mary to help with the chores. Jesus says: *"Martha, Martha, you are anxious and troubled about many things, but one thing is necessary. Mary has chosen the good portion..."*[209] My friend told me that it took his marriage to remind him that God has to be first, and that nothing will ultimately satisfy like Jesus. He had put far too many expectations for happiness on his marriage and dear wife.

Marriage will teach us and bring us much joy. It will also quickly remind us that even a beautiful marriage is not the final aim or satisfaction. C. S. Lewis wrote, *"Aim at Heaven, and you will get Earth 'thrown in': aim at Earth, and you will get neither."*[210] Your marriage will not ultimately fulfill who you are. If you put the ultimate expectation on your spouse to fulfill you, you will throw a pathology into your marriage that will need healing.

Before I was married, I enjoyed the relative autonomy of single life. I would ask God, "What is Your will for me this week, month, year?" Life was simple. On the surface, I seemed like a genuinely okay Christian guy. I thought I was a nice guy. It hadn't occurred to me that I was selfish. I was happy serving me, and trying to serve God, but my marriage changed that. Now I had to ask God: "What is Your will in light of my responsibility for Michelle, and eventually our whole family?" My decisions were not just about me; they were affecting others. Again, all these

---

[209] Luke 10:38-42.
[210] C. S. Lewis, *Mere Christianity*, p. 134.

decisions were made with the help of Michelle. Even to this day, we rarely spend much money without consulting each other and the checkbook.

> My decisions were not just about me...

As a single man, I was concerned that family responsibility would be a hardship. As our children are now grown, I realized raising a family was the most essential education I could have. All these family "sacrifices" were a blessing. Tim Keller writes:

> *"Then the Bible says that human beings were made in God's image. That means, among other things, that we were created to worship and live for God's glory, not our own. We were made to serve God and others. That means paradoxically that if we try to put our own happiness ahead of obedience to God, we violate our own nature and become, ultimately, miserable."[211]*

Jesus again reminds His disciples of the counterintuitive power of sacrifice:

> *"If anyone would come after me, let him deny himself and take up his cross daily and follow me. For whoever would save his life will lose it, but whoever loses his life for my sake will find it."[212]*

Dr. Jerry Root writes:

> *"Marriage is the chosen, but discomfortingly forceful, encounter between a man and a woman. It is, in fact, the very design of marriage to answer our innate loneliness with a form of profound discomfort."[213]*

When I struggle with the hard questions of faith, I find it helpful to return to our origin. Literally, go back to Genesis, and ask, "What is our purpose: how and why were we created?" Genesis chapters 1-3 unfolds our nature and purpose, both before and immediately after the human race was cursed by sin.

---

[211] Timothy Keller, *The Meaning of Marriage*, p. vi.
[212] Luke 9:23.
[213] Jerry Root, *Naked and Unashamed: A Guide to the Necessary Work of Christian Marriage*, p. 7.

Remember, "Sin breaks everything." Our restoration brings glory to our Father. Again, Dr. Root writes:

> "Before they had eaten, Adam and Eve were right in their relationship with God, and right in their relationship to the earth (their work), and right in their relationship to one another, and right in their relationship to their inner lives. But after their act of disobedience, all four of these areas were shattered. Our relationship with God is one of hiding—we hear His voice and run away. Our relationship with work is frustrated—Adam will cultivate the ground, but it will be toil, and he will produce thorns; Eve will cultivate children, but the process will also be similar toil and pain. Our relationship to one another is pained as well—Eve's desire will be for her husband, and he will rule over her—their partnership is fractured. (We can only imagine the conversations that follow for the duration of their marriage: 'You ate first!' 'You didn't say anything about it!') Lastly, Adam and Eve are broken within themselves—they experience shame in their innermost person.[214]

In a marriage that tries to honor God, it will be useful to remember the incredibly high standard God placed on marriage, and how far marriage has fallen. Likewise, God has forgiven, redeemed, and is now restoring us back to His image.[215]

FOR CONTEMPLATION:

A professor once told me, "If you wait until your motives are perfect, you will never be ready to serve the Lord." I think that is also true with marriage and family. No one has a perfect marriage or family. However, working hard to "deny thyself" and nurture your family will transform your life. By using your "talent," and honoring God with your family, you will be a refreshing example to those men and women who desperately need a Christian model of marriage and family.

---

[214] Ibid., p. 52.
[215] 2 Corinthians 3:18.

- How can you allow God to shape your life through your marriage today?
- How has hospitality shaped you spiritually?
- Whom do you know that needs to be shown hospitality this month?
- Are you opening up your home as a form of discipleship?

Chapter 20
Rugged Fusion: The Art of Synergy

"And together, as is the habit of some, but encouraging one another, and all the more as you see the Day drawing near."[216]

"The world is desperately seeking someone to follow. That they will follow someone is certain, but will that person be one who knows the way of Christ... The relevance of all that we do waits on its verdict, and in turn, the destiny of the multitudes hangs in the balance."[217]

"By its very nature, sailing is slightly enigmatic, and requires abstract thought. You cannot just press a button, and go where and whenever you like. It takes effort."[218]

Disciple-making, like sailing, is enigmatic. It requires abstract thought, and it takes effort. In the very first chapter of this book I explained that *rugged* disciple-making was the merging (like the ingredients to a great meal) of a combination of spiritual disciplines. With a queasy gut I cut loose from the dock, slipped my Yanmar diesel into reverse, and headed out of my slip in my old sailboat. My mind was racing. I did not want to hit one of the million-dollar powerboats in the slip across from me. In Britain, student drivers have a big red "L" strapped on the back of their car to indicate that a "Learner" was operating the vehicle. I was a rookie sailor on my maiden solo voyage; but alas, no red "L" was there to warn unsuspecting captains. As two yachts passed me with a casual wave, I wanted to wave one of those red "L's" at them, and warn them that I was a "Learner" and to give me a wide berth.

Motoring out of the dock, I entered the open waters on a busy Saturday afternoon, and that in itself felt like a victory.

---

[216] Hebrews 10:24, 25.
[217] Robert Emerson Coleman, *The Master Plan of Evangelism*, p. 132.
[218] David Seidman, *The Complete Sailor*, p. 4.

Being a novice sailor, I was drawing on minimal actual sailing experience. As I headed into the wind, I killed my diesel and unfurled my sails. That was my first mistake. I should not have killed the diesel until the sails were completely open. The boat drifted before I could get the sails entirely out, and I struggled to finish unfurling. The wind blew me around, and the jib needed to be switched from port to starboard. The boat badly keeled to one side, and I started asking myself what I was doing out there.

It had been a long winter of reading sailing books, and over eight months since my wife and I had taken our singular lesson on sailing. Now here I was, desperately trying to put together the skills and any muscle memory that might help me to sail the boat. Mix that equation with a north/northwesterly wind at 10-15 miles an hour in an old vessel I was just getting to know. My mind was whirling as I desperately tried to draw on my past skills from past hobbies. Sadly, there was very little transferable data in my memory bank to be useful for this new challenge.

Finally, I felt the magic of the wind filling my sails and righting the keel, only to be discouraged as I watched both sails lose their shape. I had not cinched either my mainsail or my jib properly. I watched helplessly as both sails blew out and flapped violently on their masts. It was then I remembered that my wife encouraged me to get a hobby and relax a little!

Sailing uses a cat's-cradle of skills, components, and disciplines; you need a vessel, the elements (both wind and water), and a sailor. These components can be united into an exciting force. It can also be a source of immense frustration. I watched my hands clumsily try to coil the sheets on the winch. I was frustrated by my body as I awkwardly tried to maneuver in the cockpit. What would eventually become reflexive and intuitive skills felt like momentous tasks that I was hopeless to perform. I set my mind on a course for the journey, and changed destinations a dozen times before giving up, just happy to drift. What is a simple day on the water for a seasoned sailor can be an exhausting experience for someone who is trying to pull together the limited knowledge, experience, and skill which he may or may not possess.

Now ashore after a rough docking, a kind man on the pier named Rod, a master sailor, walked over to my slip, and asked me if I needed any help. A wave of embarrassment came over me. I laughed and said: "Is it that obvious?" He was a skilled sailor, and I admired his poise on the water. Rod's boat was always tight and shipshape. I felt a wave of pride come over me, and my first reaction was to say, "Thanks, but I'm good—it's all under control." Nevertheless, I was such a poor sailor, and so humbled at my lack of skill, that I quickly stifled my pride, and gratefully, if a bit hesitantly, accepted his help.

Rod took me out on his boat, and we went out on mine. He taught me how to do the rigging, how to trim the sails, and how to navigate. We even started to race. He was a wealth of knowledge. However, it wasn't just his knowledge which he passed on to me. I also watched him captain the boat with confidence and joy, and I saw him appreciate the beauty of our surroundings. I admired his demeanor in competitions, and I saw the kindness and patience he had with other sailors in the marina. We also had great spiritual conversations. He taught me how to better disciple others.

> He taught me how to better disciple others.

Like sailing, disciple-making is the discipline of fusing together several interdisciplinary skills, experiences, and resources to create a synergy. It is the fusion of disciplines that help *rugged* disciple-makers to transform and help to mature *rugged* disciples. What seems like a simple and effortless task to you (like reading your Bible, praying, evangelizing) may seem like overwhelming exercise for your disciple.

In biochemistry, synergy is created when two or more distinct agents act together to create a result more significant than their separate effects. The opposite of synergy is "antagonism," the occurrence where two or more agents hinder one another's effects.

Fruitful disciple-making harnesses apparently unrelated principles and unites them into an influential source of power, like prayer *and* evangelism.

Steel was first made by fusing iron ore, charcoal, ash, and glass sealed in a crucible and fired in a furnace to create a stronger metal than any had known previously. Similarly, disciples are made by the fusion of Biblical principles forged in the crucible of life. If any of these components is missing, the leader cannot hope to attain the collective strength necessary for a *rugged* disciple. Perhaps this can partly explain why some who attempt disciple-making fail or create fragile disciples.

As we make disciples, we cannot pick and choose, or emphasize only one or two spiritual disciplines, and neglect others. Jesus modeled a passionate love for His Father, which was demonstrated through His discipline of prayer. Yet Jesus also modeled to His disciples His passion for souls, which was shown through His formal and informal evangelism.

Envision disciple-making as the fusion of spiritual disciplines including Bible study, prayer, evangelism, encouragement, character, grace, and stewardship. These components fuse together to create a synergy of *rugged* Christianity. We need more *rugged* Christians.

Where my sailing illustration breaks down is that we are not merely helping another person learn a skill; we are helping him to mature supernaturally. As Paul was inspired to write:

> *"Him we proclaim, warning everyone and teaching everyone with all wisdom, that we may present everyone mature in Christ. For this I toil, struggling with all his energy that he powerfully works within me."*[219]

It is not our ultimate teaching ability, knowledge, or time that eventually matures a disciple. It is the supernatural power of God working in the heart, mind, and soul of your disciple, and working through us and many others. Many disciple-makers plateau. They excel within their inherent skill but stop learning or stop depending on the supernatural power of God. Others stay on their knees; they keep developing new skills; and continue to obtain a greater depth of spiritual maturity. We want you to be a master disciple-maker.

POSTSCRIPT:

Again, like sailing, disciple-making is the discipline of fusing together several interdisciplinary skills, experiences, and resources to create a synergy. The rabbi-disciple experience was more than a classroom lecture. The passage below shows us how

---

[219] Colossians 1:28, 29.

Jesus taught and incorporated so many disciplines into His daily encounters:

> *"As Jesus passed on from there, he saw a man called Matthew sitting at the tax booth, and he said to him, 'Follow me.' And he rose and followed him. And as Jesus reclined at table in the house, behold, many tax collectors and sinners came and were reclining with Jesus and his disciples. And when the Pharisees saw this, they said to his disciples, 'Why does your teacher eat with tax collectors and sinners?' But when he heard it, he said, 'Those who are well have no need of a physician, but those who are sick. Go and learn what this means, "I desire mercy, and not sacrifice." For I came not to call the righteous, but sinners.'"*[220]

Here are a few lessons the disciples learned from this one dinner with Matthew and his friends:

Jesus modeled recruitment when He said to Matthew, "Follow me."

- Jesus modeled being unashamed to associate with "tax collectors and sinners."
- By eating with Matthew and his associates, Jesus emphasized the building of relationships.
- When the Pharisees question Jesus' behavior (eating with sinners), Jesus demonstrated His composure, character, and courage.
- Jesus used dinner as an excellent teaching opportunity.
- Jesus employed Scripture: *"Go and learn what this means, 'I desire mercy, and not sacrifice.'"*[221]
- Jesus cast vision: *"For I came not to call the righteous, but sinners."*

The day-to-day lessons that Jesus the master Disciple-maker taught His disciples were crucial to their development. This methodology of training could not have been as impactful if they were merely given in a classroom lecture. To create

---

[220] Matthew 9:9-13.
[221] Matthew 9:13; see Hosea 6:6.

rugged disciples, Jesus needed them to experience *rugged* life lessons.

This book is intended to give you a macro-tool (big picture) that can be easily transferred into your daily disciple-making approach. If I may be so grand, disciple-making is the activity of an artist possessed by the vision of perfection, who utilizing Biblical resources and spiritual warfare, endeavors to help another human to glorify God. God gives us, albeit over time, a vision, and a sense of calling. We have been endowed with specific means, and when we rise to this calling and use every *rugged* talent we have for His glory, there is an eternally *rugged* impact.

We can also choose to ignore God's calling to "Go and make disciples." If so, our life will have limited earthly meaning. The little scrap of eternal significance we make will have more consequences than the most significant achievement we can make apart from God.

> *"Now if anyone builds on the foundation with gold, silver, precious stones, wood, hay, straw—each one's work will become manifest, for the Day will disclose it, because it will be revealed by fire, and the fire will test what sort of work each one has done. If the work that anyone has built on the foundation survives, he will receive a reward. If anyone's work is burned up, he will suffer loss, though he himself will be saved, but only as through fire."[222]*

Can You Really Predict the Future?

In a high school assembly, I was speaking on leadership and how Jesus was the world's most effective and most influential Leader. I stated that Jesus' followers would go places and do things that they had never dreamed of doing. I gave the example of Peter, who walked on water, at least for a few steps… in a storm! Eventually, however, Peter started sinking and cried out: "Save me."[223] I continued by saying it was only then that Jesus rescued Peter. I then drove the point home by stating that we

---

[222] 1 Corinthians 3:12-15.
[223] Matthew 14:22-33.

all in some way need to cry out: "Save me." I assured all within the sound of my voice that Jesus would indeed save all who cried out to Him.

Peter's friends, who didn't initially have the courage to step out, stayed in the boat, and yet, they would later go on to change the world. I told the assembly they should pick their friends wisely so they, too, could go and make a global impact. I added that if they were to show me their friends, I would be able to show them their future.

Later in the assembly, during a time of questions and answers, a young man asked: "Can you really see the future?" I affirmed I could. I stated that global predictions were far easier to predict than most pundits let on and confirmed with conclusive evidence that we were all going to die. In fact, the global death rate in recent years is 100%.

Interestingly, we humans are the only creatures on the planet that know they are going to die. The strange thing is that most of us live like the lower forms of animals, and rarely contemplate our own mortality. To be even more accurate, we can state that only our bodies die, and our reality, our very soul, goes either to heaven or hell. What we cannot predict is our journey.

Even if you get in the boat with Christ, your voyage with Him is notoriously unpredictable. Yet, I have recognized that those people that surround themselves with men and women that will help them navigate life are much more likely to become *rugged* Christians. Lastly, I told the young man that I had also noticed that those people that want to help others to navigate this world quite often encounter a *rugged* adventure.

> *"For we must all appear before the judgment seat of Christ, so that each one may receive what is due for what he has done in the body, whether good or evil. Therefore, knowing the fear of the Lord, we persuade others. But what we are is known to God, and I hope it is known also to your conscience."*[224]

Don't miss the point!

---

[224] 2 Corinthians 5:10, 11.

Lastly, I hear some say: "Steve, you have been so blessed to have so many amazing people in your life. Where are such people? I can't seem to find them." Granted, I have been blessed to have so many men and women disciple me. Yes, they may be hard to find, but keep seeking. I encourage you to keep reaching out to mature Christians you respect and ask them to disciple you; but don't miss the point! I wrote this because you can be one of those amazing people in another person's life. **"Go"...** *Rugged...*

> *Don't miss the point! "Go"... Rugged...*

ABOUT THE AUTHOR

Connor is President/CEO of Sports Outreach International, a nonprofit which pioneers sports ministry around the world. Connor has played, coached, and has been a chaplain on every level of sport and in multiple countries. Steve is a frequent speaker and has addressed various audiences from Nascar's Joe Gibbs Racing to members of the royal family in the United Kingdom.

He has a background in sport, NAIA Two-time All American, and a "short and un-illustrious" career with the Historic Chicago Bears and Los Angeles Rams. He has published ten books and has been a Global Facilitator for the ISC (International Sports Coalition, North America).

Steve and Michelle have been married for over thirty years (fifteen years living in England and Scotland); they have three children in missions. Connor was honored with his Doctorate from Azusa Pacific University.

Steve has visited over 100 countries. He has ridden motorcycles on six continents. He loves playing jazz on his 100-year-old upright bass and lacks only talent to be an accomplished musician.

CONNECT WITH STEVE:

Steve loves evangelism and disciple-making, especially in the local church. He would enjoy hearing from you at: steve@ruggeddiscipleship.org. Steve loves to encourage, and has spoken to several local churches, conferences, and training events around the world. He is available to enthuse, engage, and train your leadership, organization, men's ministry, team, or congregation with his storytelling and special brand of *rugged* experiences.

Made in USA - Kendallville, IN
74741_9781734500103
01.27.2022 1709